BUSINESS SCHOOL INTERNATIONALISATION IN A CHANGING WORLD

This is the Open Access edition of *Global Focus* from the European Foundation for Management Development (EFMD). *Global Focus* has become one of the most authoritative resources for in-depth analysis and updates on international management development. With features, topical reports, thought leadership and insight from leading experts from academia, business schools, companies and consultancies, this edition focuses on business school internationalisation.

This eighteenth volume focuses on the impact of Artificial Intelligence (AI), with insights into topics such as the role of AI in corporate learning by Martin Moehrle, reshaping business education using hands-on AI by Ana Freire, and whether generative AI is a threat to the world of teaching and learning by Pär Mårtensson and John Mullins. The topic of the impact of business school research is explored by Kai Peters and Howard Thomas, and Usha Haley, Cary Cooper and Andrew Jack look at societal impact through sustainable scholarship. Chapters also focus on important aspects of working in business and business schools, such as Dan Pontefract's discussion of loneliness both within and beyond the workplace and the importance of 'finding your people', and insights for developing an international scholar career presented by Miguel Córdova.

This book will be of value and interest to those working in business schools and higher education leaders, as well as policy makers and business leaders seeking insight into how management education will be shaped to support business and wider society.

Matthew Wood is Director, Operations and *Global Focus* Magazine Editor at EFMD Global.

EFMD Management Education

This series is published in collaboration with EFMD Global.

Perspectives on the Impact, Mission and Purpose of the Business School
Edited by Eric Cornuel, Thomas Howard and Matthew Wood

Business School Research
Excellence, Academic Quality and Positive Impact
Edited by Eric Cornuel, Thomas Howard and Matthew Wood

Business School Internationalisation in a Changing World
Edited by Matthew Wood

For more information about this series, please visit: www.routledge.com/EFMD-Management-Education/book-series/EFMD

Business School Internationalisation in a Changing World

Edited by Matthew Wood

Routledge
Taylor & Francis Group
LONDON AND NEW YORK

Cover design: © Jebens Design

First published 2025
by Routledge
4 Park Square, Milton Park, Abingdon, Oxon OX14 4RN

and by Routledge
605 Third Avenue, New York, NY 10158

Routledge is an imprint of the Taylor & Francis Group, an informa business

Funded by EFMD Global.

British Library Cataloguing-in-Publication Data
A catalogue record for this book is available from the British Library

Library of Congress Cataloging-in-Publication Data
A catalog record has been requested for this book

ISBN: 978-1-032-80560-3 (hbk)
ISBN: 978-1-003-50062-9 (ebk)

DOI: 10.4324/9781003500629

Designed and typeset in Roboto by Jebens Design

Contents

Global Focus
The EFMD Business Magazine
Iss.1 Vol.18 | 2024

Executive Editor
Matthew Wood / matthew.wood@efmdglobal.org

Advisory Board
Eric Cornuel
Howard Thomas
John Peters

Design & Art Direction
Jebens Design / www.jebensdesign.co.uk

Photographs & Illustrations
©Jebens Design Ltd / EFMD unless otherwise stated

Editorial & Advertising
Matthew Wood / matthew.wood@efmdglobal.org
Telephone: +32 2 629 0810

www.globalfocusmagazine.com
www.efmdglobal.org

©EFMD
Rue Gachard 88 – Box 3,
1050 Brussels, Belgium

More ways to read *Global Focus*

You can read *Global Focus* in print, online and on the move, in English, Chinese, Russian or Spanish

Go to globalfocusmagazine.com to access the online library of past issues

Your say

We are always pleased to hear your thoughts on Global Focus, and ideas on what you would like to see in future issues.

Please address comments and ideas to Matthew Wood at EFMD: matthew.wood@efmdglobal.org

17

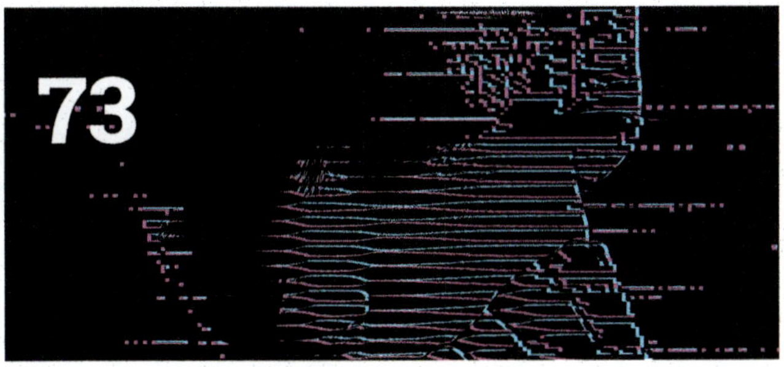
73

Business School Internationalisation in a Changing World

Exposure to different cultures and ways of doing business are important elements of business school education. In the face of major societal, environmental and technological transition, **Julie Perrin-Halot** and **Simon Mercado** examine how internationalisation is evolving and how more sustainable practices can be adopted

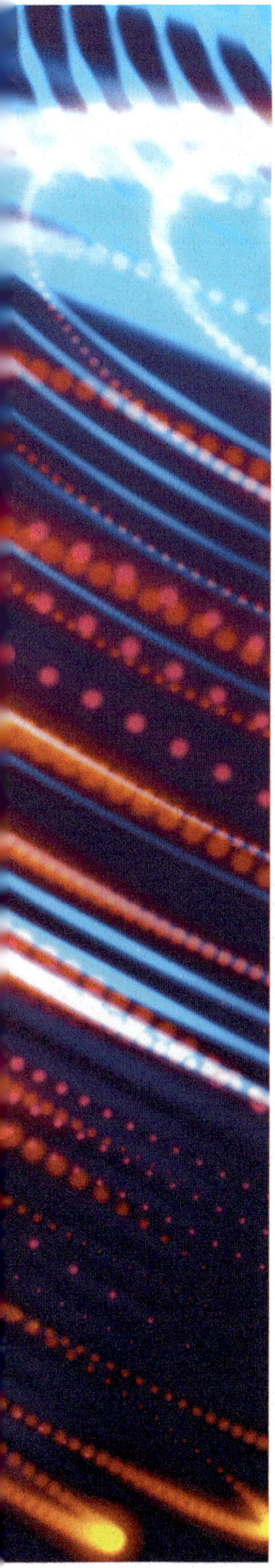

For several decades, the world's business schools have been taking a strategic approach to internationalisation. In previous articles and commentaries (e.g., Mercado & Perrin-Halot, 2018), we observed that enhanced international cooperation and capacity building stood as the most cited benefits of internationalisation at the institutional level. At the individual level, international strategies were seen widely as drivers of international learning and mobility.

Whilst these drivers remain pertinent today, the landscape has fundamentally changed and approaches to internationalisation are necessarily evolving. This evolution in the focus and character of internationalisation is taking place at a time of major societal, environmental, and technological transition. It also comes in the aftermath of the COVID-19 pandemic and in a context of heightened global instability. For many, we have entered a period of disruption and 'poly-crisis', which exposes fundamental shortcomings in our business-as-usual approaches. In higher education (HE), we are at the confluence of a world coming undone and a world reinventing itself, and there is a growing recognition that HE providers need to make a deliberate and impactful response.

Attaching to this is a critique of the last thirty years or so of sectoral internationalisation framed by such macro-level developments as the GATS (General Agreement on Trade in Services) and the Bologna Process, which delivered a more open and harmonised European Higher Education Area (EHEA). This critique includes a questioning of a global model in which close to 6 million people move across borders annually to study for a degree or degree-related credits at a heavy environmental cost. Implicit here is a questioning of what Healey calls the export education model, in which recruiting institutions (in largely wealthy countries) contribute not only to these environmentally damaging mobility flows but also to north-south inequalities and brain-drain effects (see Healey 2023).

Towards Internationalisation 2.0

All of this creates the imperative and conditions for a new paradigm in internationalisation, which we reference here as *Internationalisation 2.0*. The case could be made for putting an end to mobility and what continues to be a determined pursuit of financially-driven internationalisation in the sector. When looking at carbon emissions generated by staff and student mobility alone, there is clearly an issue with concerns raised over the environmental impact of international flights. Surveys done with students show that low-cost flights remain far more popular than the alternatives including the costlier and more onerous rail option. When concerns over north-south inequalities and coloniality are factored in, the case against internationalisation as we have known it builds convincingly.

Yet, global challenges require global solutions. To tackle the grand challenges of our time and to take a more proactive role in addressing the United Nations' Sustainable Development Goals, we need strong collaborations across national borders, industries, and organisations. We see in the data released in 2023 a marked correlation between international collaboration in research and the impact of that research, as measured through field-weighted citation impact. International education can be a powerful vehicle for enriching teaching and learning, and, for creating a more connected and humanist world. International mobility experience and other forms of international engagement play a fundamental role in creating global mindsets, in developing tolerance, curiosity and the capacity to interact and work across all types of differences. As higher education professionals, most of us agree that international and intercultural exposure and experience are an important part of a student's development and that eliminating this dimension risks doing more harm than good.

The question then becomes, how do we continue to include internationalisation as a fundamental part of our activities as an HEI while ensuring that our choices and impact are aligned with economic, societal, and environmental transitions?

The STRIVE framework

The STRIVE framework, shared in a first EFMD seminar on Internationalisation 2.0 in June 2023, proposes to bring clarity, method, and tools to the different dimensions of this question and plots a way forward for schools. The framework identifies six key priorities for future internationalisation, all of which intersect and correspond. The framework can give direction to business schools and their communities as they rethink and re-engineer internationalisation for a better world and environment. Behind the model is a view that we must strive to move beyond current business models and practices. The wordplay is naturally deliberate. Our approach emphasises the importance of a more responsible (R) and sustainable (S) internationalisation model, in which our practices are also deeply ethical (E) and inclusive (I). All of this points to more equitable collaborations and the pursuit of a more just and diverse higher education landscape. A key lever for this is a more transnational (T) approach to internationalisation in which partnerships are increasingly multilateral (one with many) rather than purely bilateral (one to one). A second is the adoption of new technological innovations and habits to promote what is widely referred to as virtual (V) internationalisation. Let us take a step into these six domains and priorities of the STRIVE framework (Figure 1).

> *...business schools must reorient their internationalisation models and direct them towards enhanced climate and biodiversity literacy*

Sustainable (S) Internationalisation

The starting point of the model, and perhaps our core proposition, is that business schools must reorient their internationalisation models and direct them towards enhanced climate and biodiversity literacy, as well as to more sustainable business models and practices. On the one hand, sustainable internationalisation implies education and research that can help address the myriad of challenges around climate change and biodiversity, bringing in knowledge and science from outside of the traditional business disciplines. On the other hand, it demands that schools themselves are walking the talk through greener policy and action. This change in institutional behaviour is difficult to realise in the context of a continuing commitment to physical mobility of persons, but there are certain actions that

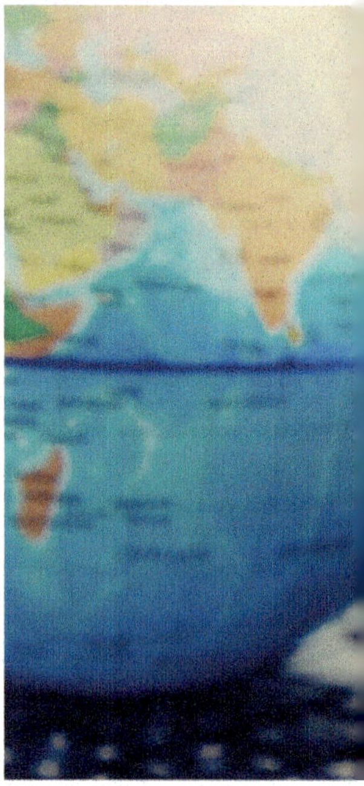

Figure 1. The STRIVE framework

1-2-1

Already, business schools have moved beyond an era of bilateral (1-2-1) cooperation agreements into more diverse and multilateral networks

can and must follow, such as focusing more on longer-term mobility, virtual supplements to physical mobility, and that which delivers the highest value-add. Other options include the introduction of carbon passport schemes (limiting total travel), systemic C02 footprint measurement and quota setting, and/or carbon emission off-set initiatives. Whatever the approach or methodology, attacking the environmental cost of staff and student mobility is an important step, which should involve environmental plans to minimise the carbon footprint of international travel and wider international engagement. To help schools address these imperatives, potential reference points include the spectrum of UN Sustainable Development Goals, peer-generated guidelines such as the net-zero promoting CANIE Accord, Green ERASMUS directives, and other national and international frameworks.

Sustainable internationalisation presupposes that business schools are using internationalisation to create greater awareness among their stakeholders around the broader societal, environmental, and economic issues that the planet and its populations are facing. In its widest sense, sustainable internationalisation means that those engaging are fully cognisant of the impact of their choices of location, of mode of travel, and of the lifestyle they are leading in their destination of choice. It involves critical thinking about cultural, developmental and economic differences and pushes participants to reflect on how for each personal internationalisation project, they can create positive value and impact.

Transnational (T) Internationalisation

Already, business schools have moved beyond an era of bilateral (1-2-1) cooperation agreements into more diverse and multilateral networks. These range from funded consortia projects through to common interest networks such as RRBM, EQUAL, PRIME, GBSN and GRLI. In terms of their ability to deliver joint actions (in education and research) and intelligence sharing, these networks are paving the way to new initiatives and means of understanding and addressing our grand challenges.

In our view, business schools will need more engagements of this type to realise their missions, to secure funding, and to address the issues they should be tackling. They should effect internal changes that allow them to pool resources, credits, and capacities with other institutions more easily. In all such cases, we see the potential in combined expertise and resources for imagining new scenarios and creating the conditions necessary for making impactful and lasting change.

It is noteworthy here that the European Commission has prioritised transnational engagement through new European University Alliances focused on inter-university degrees, campuses, and research projects. These are envisaged to involve more than 500 HEIs in 60 or more groupings. The broad idea is to strengthen the international dimension of higher education and research and to empower universities as key actors of change in the twin green and digital transitions.

Responsible (R) Internationalisation

Our first interpretation of the concept of responsible internationalisation is that international actions, programmes and projects should support institutional commitment to social responsibility and equity. In the same vein, research and education should focus where possible on responsible citizenship and leadership. Responsible internationalisation also requires an explicit focus on inclusion and ethical behaviour which we address in subsequent sections.

Institutions can play their part by creating systems to ensure that students and staff on mobility are aware of the carbon costs of their activity

Responsible internationalisation also entails a sense of personal responsibility for each individual engaged in an international activity, with reflexes around impact assessment and evaluation. Institutions can play their part by creating systems to ensure that students and staff on mobility are aware of the carbon costs of their activity and have options available to reduce that as far as possible. They should also be primed to identify and seize opportunities for positive impact wherever they go.

Increasingly important and often overlooked is the fact that institutions have a responsibility for the safety and well-being of their inbound and outbound mobile participants. In the most basic sense, risk management and mitigation should be the institutional norm with specific attention to the relationship between risk and international activity. Systems and processes must be in place for rapid and effective action if a student or staff member on mobility for the school is in a situation that threatens their health or safety.

Inclusive (I) Internationalisation

An inclusive approach must correct the, sometimes exclusive, nature of current internationalisation policies and practices. For example, degree- or credit-based international student mobility is a socially selective process, whereby students from lower socio-economic backgrounds are less likely to participate. As put by two leading commentators, "while credit and degree mobility is increasing globally, this billion-dollar industry reaches only a small student elite, leaving 99% of the world's student population behind" (de Wit and Jones, 2018:16).

With a focus on greater equity of access, inclusive internationalisation must look to bring international education and experience to a broader group of students, lowering costs and access barriers. Rather than bringing international learners across borders at high cost, institutions can move to local markets to provide their courses in country or online. In terms of more traditional mobility, institutions must also look at financial support for international students and at their pricing strategies, which too often impose discriminatory fees and/or higher prices on international students versus their domestic counterparts.

The inclusive internationalisation agenda also includes the development of effective strategies for internationalisation at home (IaH) focused on international activities at the home institution for staff and students who do not travel. It also requires that business schools promote, harness, and respond to diversity in learner and staff populations, recognising and validating different backgrounds and perspectives. Here, challenges range from inclusive curriculum design through to inclusive teaching, learning and assessment strategies.

Virtual (V) Internationalisation

Internationalisation of higher education has been naturally affected by the development of digital technologies and e-learning markets. Online learning already had an established place in the global market before the COVID-19 pandemic turbo-charged technology adoption and virtual internationalisation. Virtual pathways to internationalisation can include online distance learning (at least that part of which takes place across borders), virtual exchange, and online collaborative international learning (COIL). What has become apparent is that virtual exchange and mobility can supplement and at times replace physical mobility, taking a place in hybrid mobility strategies that deliver internationalisation to a wider population and help institutions to reduce their carbon footprint. Of course, it is doubtful that virtual exchange and mobility can replace in-person experiences in terms of cultural immersion and personal development. That said, VE can offer students authentic intercultural learning experiences and can contribute to the more sustainable and inclusive internationalisation approaches we advocate.

Ethical & Equitable (E) Internationalisation

The span of considerations here is vast. At the highest level, institutions will need to make difficult decisions about the ethics of engaging with entities in specific states and regions subject to international censure or restrictions. In recent times, business schools have faced challenges of this type within their partnership portfolios (e.g., links to Russian business schools and their partners). Complex issues surround partnering in countries with strongly conflicting value sets. For certain, business schools and their parent institutions must engage in internationalisation that prioritises the well-being, equity, and ethical considerations of all those involved, both from the school side as well as in the host location. This is a values-based approach and must be built on many of the elements shared throughout the framework above. Ethical and equitable internationalisation means that schools approach partnerships where values are aligned, and cultural sensitivity is practiced in both directions. It also means providing equal opportunity to all those wanting to participate in internationalisation activities. Accountability and transparency are critical as are strategies to mitigate potential negative impact - codes of ethics have their place here.

An ethical approach to internationalisation also includes a commitment to protecting the rights and interests of international students as cross-border subjects prone to specific risks. It may not be possible or easy to de-risk the sectoral ecosystem for all parties, but some concrete measures are necessary to ensure such things as personal data protection and the quality of intermediaries. The international recruitment agency system is one area of specific concern. The sales agent-student-HEI relationship is a complex one and whilst HEIs can work successfully and transparently with sales agents validating their quality and regulating many of their actions, concerns are building across the industry over the use of sub-agents and agent aggregators. Here, reputable institutions should move with care and act with full transparency. An ethical approach to internationalisation also means that institutions should distance themselves from any form of mis-advertising or mis-selling, however competitive the landscape. Question marks exist over the ethicality of everything from pay-and-play rankings to the bamboozling of student buyers with claims around graduate employability rates often not fully informed by data on international student placement.

International and intercultural awareness and sensitivity are more important than ever

Our STRIVE framework can be utilised to revisit existing practices and define future models and strategies. The key to this framework is its inherent transversality, both in terms of a comprehensive approach to internationalisation and the requirement for collaboration between different parts of the institution. Internationalisation should be 'connective tissue' cutting across activities, disciplines, and departments. Only through this transversal approach will the six elements come to life and deliver needed results.

The next edition of the workshop on Rethinking your International Strategy will take place in June 2024. More details can be found https://events.efmdglobal.org/events/2024-re-thinking-internationalisation/, or email Marketa Dvorackova at marketa.dvorackova@efmdglobal.org for further information.

Conclusion

We remain committed to the preservation of internationalisation within our business school activities. International and intercultural awareness and sensitivity are more important than ever. Nonetheless, yesterday's practices need rethinking to ensure that tomorrow's internationalisation addresses the grand challenges of our time and focuses on positive societal impact. The degree to which this constitutes a real and lasting paradigm shift (Internationalisation 2.0?) will reveal itself over time. It is at least encouraging to see the genuine efforts of our schools to be agents of positive change and to reimagine internationalisation.

About the Authors

Julie Perrin-Halot is Associate Dean/Director Accreditations, Sustainability and Strategic Planning at Grenoble Ecole de Management, Grenoble, France.

Professor Simon Mercado is Executive Vice President and Dean for Global Affairs, ESCP Business School.

References:

De Wit, H. and E. Jones (2018) Inclusive Internationalization: Improving Access and Equity, International Higher Education, 94, *pp.16-18.*

Healey, N.M. (2023) Reinventing International Higher Education for a Socially Just, Sustainable World, Perspectives: Policy & Practice in Higher Education, 27*(4) pp.169-178.*

Mercado, S.A. and J. Perrin-Halot (2019) A Strategy for Business School Internationalisation, BGA/Business Impact, issue 01 *pp.26-29*

Mercado, S.A. and J. Perrin-Halot (2017) Making International Collaboration Work, EFMD Global Focus, 11*(3) pp.42-45.*

Work-Life Bloom

Loneliness both within and beyond the workplace is rife. **Dan Pontefract** discusses ways to help mitigate this and the importance of 'finding your people'

> *The current leaders revel in the opportunity to put on festive aprons and ridiculously oversized oven mitts*

With all due respect to the 1980s Norwegian band, you're bound to have a few "a-ha" moments when you change roles and companies. I joined Canadian corporate giant TELUS in late 2008, a few months after leaving SAP. One of the first events I participated in at TELUS was the annual Retirees Holiday Lunch. Despite its current-day international prowess across multiple business lines, TELUS started in 1904 as a British Columbia–based, publicly run telecommunications company. Given its history, telecom retirees are an essential part of the culture.

The Retirees Holiday Lunch is just as you might expect. In a large room that accommodates hundreds of people, former TELUS team members arrive just before noon to be feted and served by current executives and leaders. The meal is turkey—with all the trimmings—complemented by holiday goodies, eggnog, and hot chocolate. The current leaders revel in the opportunity to put on festive aprons and ridiculously oversized oven mitts, taking orders and delivering hot plates to the retirees' liking. Lovely thank-you gifts are distributed at the end of the shindig.

During my inaugural Holiday Lunch, I had a conversation with an older woman that sticks with me to this day. It was a festive "a-ha" moment, a gift that keeps giving.

After a few small-talk questions and answers, I realised I was talking to a 40-year veteran of the company. She was a former director who had held several different roles and responsibilities over her tenure. She had been retired for over a decade. Somehow, we then got onto the subject of networks and relationships. I'm paraphrasing, but the end of the conversation went something like the following:

"I love coming to this lunch every year. It reminds me how important my friends were to me at BC Tel [former name of TELUS]. I was busy but happy. There was a lot going on. But I was never bored, never lonely."

And then, without prompting, she offered me some advice, knowing I had only been at the company for about six weeks:

"Find your people: it's the best thing you'll ever do."

I often think about that exchange. It regularly makes me wonder if today's leaders fully comprehend how important it is for team members to *find their people*. Perhaps more significantly, are leaders aware of the impact they can have when they help to create such an outcome?

Research suggests, however, that large swathes of people are lonely. Many individuals have no network, not even a small one. We might construe loneliness as the opposite of finding your people. If a person doesn't have a vibrant network—when there are no strong relationship ties in their orbit—the chances for loneliness increase. If strong ties are lacking, the likelihood of the next tier of contacts—oftentimes referred to as one's weak ties based on the work in 1973 of Stanford sociologist Mark Granovetter—dramatically diminishes, too.

Not only does loneliness create negative consequences in one's life, but it also creates deleterious workplace effects. The whole situation is about as stimulating as occupying the middle seat on an airplane, sandwiched between two obnoxiously intoxicated first-time flyers during a five-hour flight. It's that bad.

Nobel Prize winners Daniel Kahneman and Angus Deaton discovered through their 2010 research, for example, that loneliness was one of the top factors preventing life happiness and satisfaction. Unsurprisingly, people who are lonely demonstrate a high incidence of sadness, stress, and anxiety. In addition, research by the University of Chicago psychologist John Cacioppo in 2014 suggested that loneliness can increase an older person's chances of premature death by 14%.

From a work perspective, in a 2022 study of several hundred hotel employees, researchers showed that workplace loneliness leads to psychological detachment from peoples' jobs. The research also revealed that workplace loneliness contributes to emotional exhaustion, adversely affecting the home front. A similar 2020 study in New Delhi found that loneliness at work "was negatively associated with psychological well-being and self-esteem" and that managers suffering from loneliness at work reported "increased feelings of work alienation." Maybe Paul McCartney was onto something when he wrote the song 'No More Lonely Nights'.

As if things weren't bad enough, the pandemic has done us no favours on the loneliness front. For many workers in roles not deemed essential or operated from the frontline, the shift to a home-based office was swift and even distressing. Steven Van Cohen and Ryan Jenkins, who wrote the 2022 book *Connectable*, found that 72% of all global workers experience loneliness monthly, and a shocking 55% are lonely at least weekly. As the loneliness numbers continue to increase and strong and weak tie relationships plunge, research firms have assessed the costs.

> Wherever you look, loneliness and a lack of relationships cost organisations billions

A massive 2017 study of thousands of UK-based employees conducted by New Economics Research indicated that loneliness costs employers roughly £2.5 billion annually. Cigna, a US healthcare and insurance company, suggests loneliness costs US-based employers more than US$154 billion annually in stress-related absenteeism. The Bankwest Curtin Economics Centre says it costs Australian employers AU$2.7 billion. Wherever you look, loneliness and a lack of relationships cost organisations billions. It's like an omnipresent dust cloud that we just can't reach.

Incidentally, in global research that I conducted while writing my book, *Work-Life Bloom*, I discovered that a large proportion of leaders (73%) and non-leaders (59%) polled also believe that relationships are an important element of one's ability to function positively. Incidentally, male and female participants polled identically at 69%, and there was no discernible difference between Gen Z, Millennials, Gen X, and Baby Boomers. Between 68% and 70% of each generation surveyed on the topic responded that meaningful relationships were important.

43%

My research suggested only 43% of leaders felt that their current employer had helped them develop their network and relationships, which is relatively feeble

If relationships, and thus a robust network of strong and weak ties, are essential to a majority of team members, I maintain that leaders bear partial responsibility for nurturing relationships. Not only are relationships good for business, but they also combat loneliness and improve employee performance. Furthermore, a strong network can create a built-in support network for the inevitable times of life and work dodginess.

However, the sad reality that I discovered in my research is that leaders are not creating the conditions for relationships and networks to form. My research suggested only 43% of leaders felt that their current employer had helped them develop their network and relationships, which is relatively feeble. The situation is positively dire for non-leaders. A paltry 23% believed they were being provided with above-average or significant help in this area.

In 2018 - long before COVID-19 took over our lives - the UK Government created a Ministry of Loneliness in response to the loneliness crisis. It has been in operation ever since. Its purpose is clear: "Supporting people to have meaningful social relationships is not just crucial to people's physical and mental health. It also affects their engagement in the workplace and wider community cohesion." It's looking out for both the wellness of its citizens (life) and the organisations that employ them (work). I'd go so far as to say the Ministry of Loneliness could be considered one of the first groups to debunk the anachronistic term 'work-life balance'. There is no balance between work and life if we are lonely and our relationships are miniscule.

A few other people are also trying to fix this loneliness and relationship plight. Aaron Hurst is the author of *The Purpose Economy* and the founder of consulting firm Imperative, which believes "meaningful human connection at work is the key to unlocking transformational benefits both to the business and individual employees." Hurst is one of the good guys doing good things to help solve the above-mentioned predicament.

During our discussion on my *Leadership NOW* programme, Hurst pointed out that leaders must take responsibility for getting employees out of their loneliness cycle. In addition, he's adamant that leaders must help their team members by encouraging them to have meaningful relationships.

"At the junior level, a lot of it is tied to how we design jobs; all the interactions are transactional, and there's no real place for human interaction in the workplace anymore," said Hurst. "It's all transactional interaction. As you get more senior, there is actually more human interaction."

It's a salient point. Leaders are likely very busy and in multiple meetings with different people daily while also possessing a vast network of LinkedIn contacts. The same may not be accurate for team members. It might do leaders some good to check in with their team to see just how wide and deep their networks are, not only to help combat loneliness but also to build up team members' self-esteem, access to information, and sense of meaning. That, in turn, can help eliminate potential sadness, stress, anxiety, and exhaustion at work and home.

"We are wired to be naturally drawn to and thrive when we are with other people and where we feel protected by the group," Hurst said. "We are optimised neurologically to crave that, and when we don't have it, we start to shut down and operate out of fear. It's when you feel like you are part of a group of people, where it's meeting your neurological need for a tribe. And when you don't have that, you start to move into an 'us versus them' mentality, losing empathy and shutting down your willingness to take risks. Unfortunately, I think that's happened in the workplace, and the pandemic exacerbated it."

In today's fast-paced world of rapidly advancing changes, creating space for human conversations and connections is critical, especially in the workplace. Leaders must acknowledge that networks and relationships are vital components of team members' well-being. When those components are flourishing, so will the organisation and the individual.

Obviously, you are not the UK Government (unless you are reading this column and are, in fact, part of the UK Government), so you're likely not about to set up a Department of Loneliness at your organisation.

It is clear that social community has declined over the past several years and that networks - proper strong ties - have been decimated. With that decline comes both concern and opportunity. Leaders ought to be concerned because a lonely person in life is likely to be a lonely worker. And, as we've discovered, loneliness is a costly expense. Leaders may argue that being connected to a community of workplace peers is a given. Being employed is enough.

I counter-argue that when leaders treat the workplace as a social community—when building networks becomes a leadership priority—far greater benefits will accrue for team members and the organisation.

gf

About the Author

Dan Pontefract is a leadership strategist and author of Work-Life Bloom: How to Nurture a Team That Flourishes.

The European Business School Sector: Phoenix Rising from the Ashes?

Despite the primacy of US business schools and the emergence of those in Asia, European business schools are undergoing a resurgence. By **Ansgar Richter**

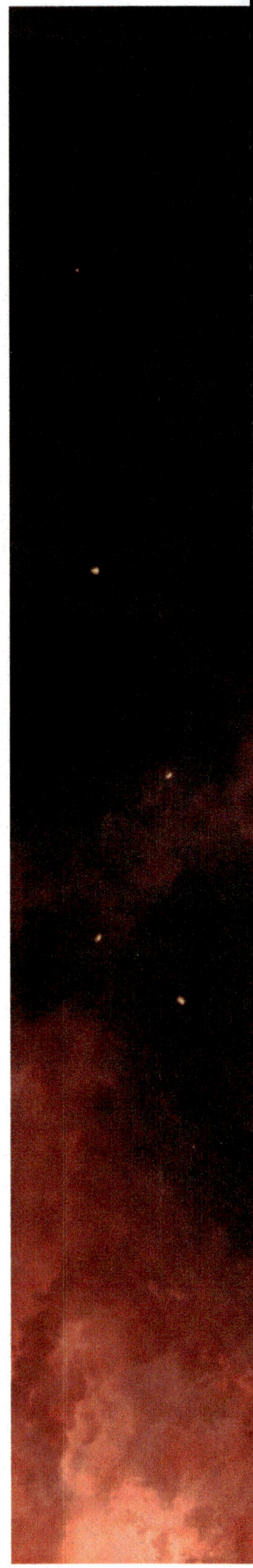

Over the past 25 years, leaders of business schools in Europe have been through a roller coaster of developments. When the *Financial Times* published its first Global MBA ranking in 1999, only eight of the 50 schools contained on that list were from continental Europe, another eight from the UK, and the remaining 34 from North America. The list did not include a single school from Germany, Austria, Italy, Belgium, or any of the Scandinavian countries. The concern was that the US schools, with their established strengths in top-notch executive education, richly funded endowments, global brand recognition and the capacity to attract the brightest faculty at the cutting edge of intellectual development, would outcompete the continental European management education sector.[1] The plethora of education systems in European countries with their fragmented regulatory environments, their reliance on evenly distributed public, thinly-spread funding, and the multiplicity of stakeholder objectives making the pursuit of any strategic growth objective difficult, was seen as a major barrier to the development of a strong continental European business school sector.

With the internet craze and the start-up wave in the early 2000s, students and young academics became ever more eager to join the entrepreneurial culture found on the shores of North America. If there was any competitive threat to these schools, it would come from the rise of business schools in Asia, and a select few other emerging economies. The success of these 'new kids on the block' would be driven by economic growth, strategic ambition, and powerful government support. Sure enough, the expanded FT Global MBA ranking in 2000 included the first Asian business school. Little surprise then that in the mid-2000s, the proportion of schools from continental Europe among the top 100 MBA providers on the FT list was below that seen in the original 1999 list.

However, a closer look at the development of the continental European business school sector since then suggests greater resilience than was considered likely those 20 years ago. For what it is worth, according to the FT MBA ranking, in 2023 there were 23 MBA programmes offered by continental European institutions among the global 100, a remarkable increase considering the simultaneous rise of programmes offered by Asian (chiefly Chinese, Indian and Singaporean) business schools (see Figure 1). The increase is even more noticeable from the FT's Executive MBA (EMBA) rankings. Whereas in 2013, 20 EMBA programmes were delivered by the leading schools in continental Europe, by 2023 this number had risen to 30 (see Figure 2). In the case of both the MBA and the EMBA rankings, the stronger position of continental European business schools was accompanied by a proportionate decline in the number of schools from North America. These rankings now include schools from a more diverse set of European countries, with those from France, Spain, Germany, the Netherlands and Switzerland being the ones with multiple entries on a regular basis.

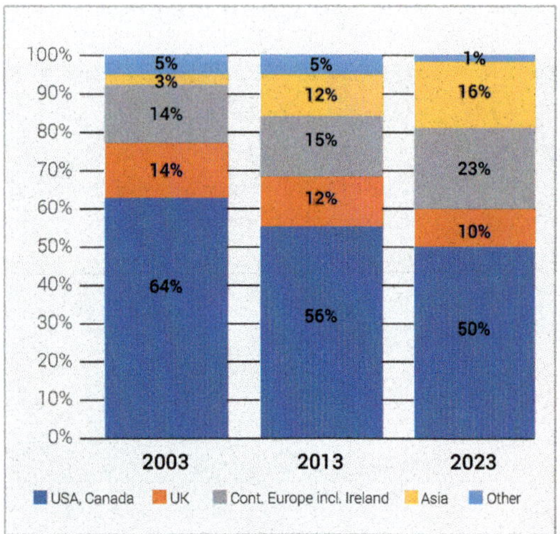

Figure 1. FT Global MBA ranking

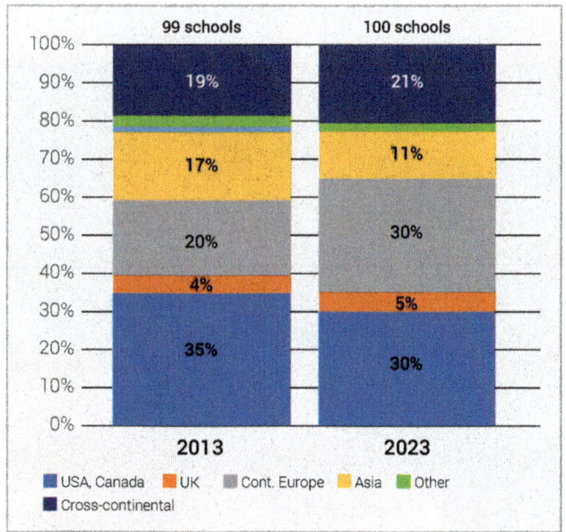

Figure 2. FT Global EMBA ranking

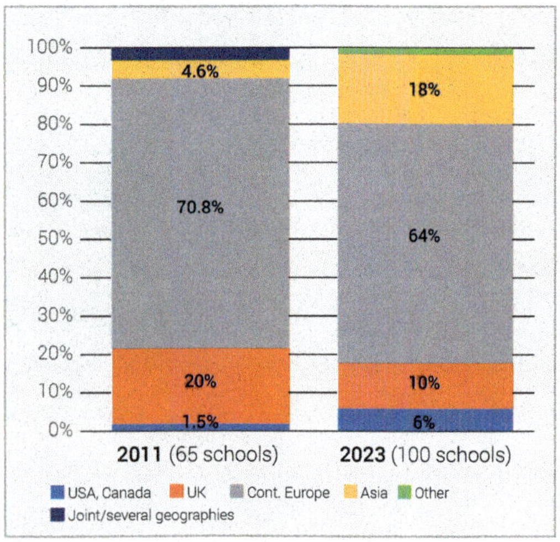

Figure 3. FT Masters in Management ranking

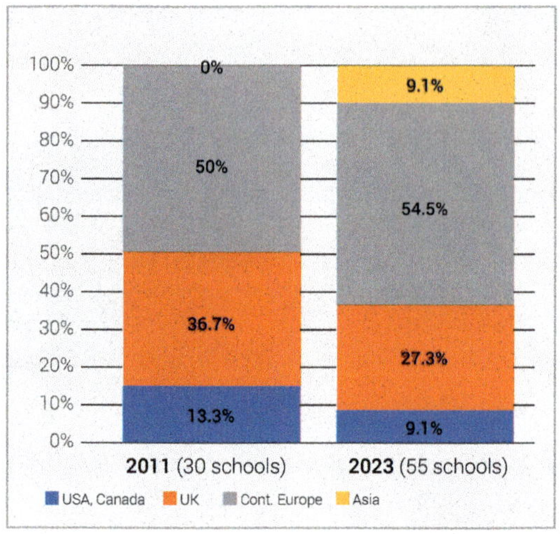

Figure 4. FT Masters in Finance ranking (pre-experience)

One could assume that with respect to MBA and EMBA programmes – widely considered quintessentially 'American' inventions – European institutions have just been playing catch-up. However, an analysis of the more 'European' Masters in Management programmes that were widely introduced in the wake of the Bologna Process reforms from the late 1990s onwards, shows that continental European institutions have lost only a modest share of the market represented in the FT rankings; and with respect to pre-experience Masters in Finance programmes, European schools have even grown their position (see Figures 3 and 4). What is particularly noteworthy in both cases is the decline in the proportion of UK-based schools. While British institutions continue to capture an outsized share of the global MSc market, their position among the most highly rated business schools appears to have suffered.

Of course, programme-based rankings offer only a very partial view of the competitive situation, and the Financial Times pays attention to a very particular mix of factors that are all subject to extensive debate. However, there are other indicators as well suggesting that continental European schools are gaining ground, if gradually so. For example, in the research area, the ranking of the top 100 institutions published by the Naveen Jindal School at the University of Texas at Dallas (UTD) included nine institutions from continental Europe in 2023, as compared to just three in 2005 (see Figure 5). In this ranking, British institutions have also increased their position strongly. The ranking is based on the number of journal articles in the so-called UTD list of journals. With just 24 journals on that list, it is widely considered to be the most restrictive list of leading journals in management, marketing,

One could assume that with respect to MBA and EMBA programmes – widely considered quintessentially 'American' inventions – European institutions have just been playing catch-up

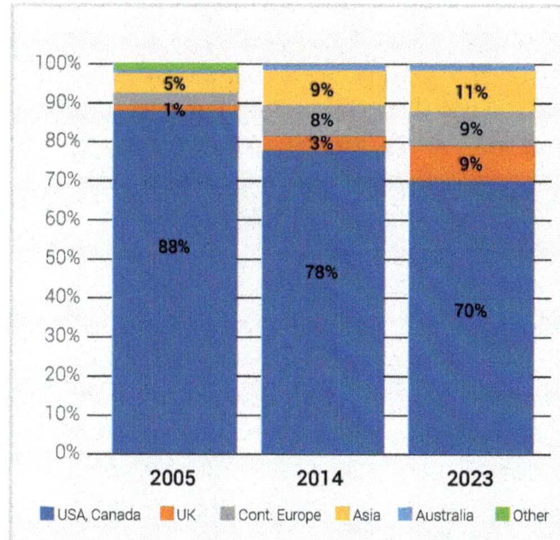

Figure 5. UTD ranking top 100 business schools

operations, finance and economics. In order to get included, an institution has to maintain a strong cadre of academics across several research fields who publish regularly in these journals – having just a handful of stars in a narrowly defined research area won't get a school there. Being included in the list of top 100 UTD research institutions is thus a sign of a strong and pervasive research environment that continuously attracts and retains top researchers. The 70 institutions from North America that are included on the list as of 2023 still dwarf the just 18 schools from Europe (nine from continental Europe, and another nine from the UK), making it too early to speak of a European renaissance in business and management research. Nevertheless, it is clear that there is a gradual shift taking place, with Asia emerging, and Europe re-emerging, as competitors to challenge America's dominance. Many more qualitative indicators, such as the greater role played by Europeans in editorial roles in academic associations and in leading journals, point in a similar direction.

Critics may argue that the indicators used above are simply the wrong ones to look at. Rankings do not do justice to the richness of management education models. The criteria that they employ may be exactly the wrong ones. By highlighting institutions that make it onto a list, they hide those that do not. They also contribute to what organisation scholars call 'isomorphism' – the tendency for organisations to look alike, at the expense of differentiation, creativity, and innovation. Even at the established schools, many stakeholders lament the 'rankings tyranny', exhorting deans to allow themselves to break out of the mental straightjacket imposed by them. Exciting and transformational developments in the business school world often come from unexpected sources - smaller institutions that innovate their programmes, technology players that offer completely new value propositions, management departments in larger universities that capitalise in unique ways on pursuing cross- and interdisciplinary research agendas, and many more.

These criticisms are legitimate however, the point of the above analysis of rankings data is a different, and much simpler one. It just indicates that concerns over whether continental European business schools have lost whatever little ground they still had those 20 years ago, are overblown. The established big-brand institutions in North America and the UK, and the new competitors from Asia, have not pushed European schools off the global competitive playing field entirely, as had been feared. Many business schools in continental Europe have undergone massive change processes leaving them stronger than they were before. What have they done well?

The first thing to note is that the overall political integration in the EU has been beneficial for higher education in the region. The Bologna Process has provided a common framework for degree programmes, the mobility of faculty and students within the block has become significantly easier, and initiatives such as the Erasmus+ programme have been hugely successful. Clearly, not all institutions have capitalised to the same extent on the emergence of a pan-European market for education. Nevertheless, the overall development has been a positive one.

Second, many continental European institutions have become more intentional about their development. They have exposed themselves to the scrutiny of (multiple) quality assurance and accreditation processes that have forced them to sharpen their strategies and explain themselves to their stakeholders. They have paid attention to an increasing number of dimensions of their work: pre- and post-experience education, knowledge development and dissemination, engagement and impact, faculty and staff development, to mention just the most salient ones. Strategic institutional development begins with identifying what it is that you aim to achieve, rather than to simply go about doing 'stuff' on the assumption that your existence is guaranteed. There are lots of schools in Europe, in particular in the public sector, that have not shed those old-fashioned attitudes. Many others, however, have begun to ask themselves what it is that they want to be really good at, and have implemented strategies to achieve these objectives.

Strategic institutional development begins with identifying what it is that you aim to achieve

At the same time, many continental European institutions have resisted the kind of dependency on tuition fees from 'overseas' students seen at some UK and US-based business schools. Income from fee-paying students can certainly provide institutions with the means to make strategic investments. However, it is also widely known that a lot of university-based business schools in the UK and the US are not entirely free to utilise this income for their own development, but that it is needed to cross-finance other parts of their parent institutions. An over-reliance on such fees can also constrain the choices a school would otherwise make (e.g., in terms of admission standards), and thus become a burden. Some continental European schools have fallen into the same trap, but the problem has been less widespread.

> *Building a research culture takes many years, perhaps decades, but it is encouraging to see it emerging*

Fourth, the idea that industry support is needed for business schools to develop, while successful business schools can be beneficial for the corporate ecosystem of which they are a part, has gradually taken hold in continental Europe. This has not only given rise to additional sources of income (e.g., from executive education), it has also opened doors for increased cooperation, fresh ideas, and a more entrepreneurial culture at many European business schools. Take the example of the development of business schools that are affiliated with the Chambers of Commerce and Industry in France. In other places, business schools have become integral parts of the entrepreneurial and start-up scene in their respective countries. In some places, private donors with a corporate or entrepreneurial background have also begun to create large endowments for new or extensions of existing business schools in ways that a few decades ago seemed unimaginable; witness the new technology campus in Heilbronn with which the Dieter Schwarz Stiftung has endowed the Technical University of Munich. These new developments have given other institutions incentives to sharpen their own game, too.

Finally, many continental European business schools have begun to improve the research environments that help to attract and retain the best faculty. A lot of them have revamped their PhD programmes, established research infrastructures that facilitate cutting-edge work, and introduced more demanding, but also more competitive, career models for their academics. At the same time, they have had a close eye on the impact their research is making. Most importantly, they have recruited faculty who are at the core of this research culture. Building a research culture takes many years, perhaps decades, but it is encouraging to see it emerging.

The future of European institutions among the world's top business schools is far from guaranteed, and maybe there are more important questions to be asked e.g. regarding the future centres of management education in Africa and Latin America. Nevertheless, there are positive lessons to be learned from the developments sketched above. The business school world is a multipolar one, and this is something to be cherished.

gf

About the Author

Ansgar Richter is Vice President of Academic Affairs at the Frankfurt School of Finance & Management, Germany

Footnote:

1 *See also Eric Cornuel: University Challenge. EFMD Global Focus, Vol. 1, No. 1, 2007, pp. 10-14.*

The Role of Alumni in the Development of their University

Thomas Bieger outlines the nature of alumni relationships and looks at how they can be capitalised on for mutual benefit

Every dean would agree that alumni are one of the most important stakeholders and resources for their university. However, the type of alumni relations, the institutionalisation of these relations, and the instruments and events used, vary between different schools and their contexts. At the same time, challenges like dealing with younger generations of graduates or keeping track of a more mobile alumni community seem to be common. As part of its 125-year programme, the University of St. Gallen organised a conference on alumni relations, bringing together representatives and perspectives from some of its partner universities: WU - University of Economics and Business Vienna, the WHU – Otto Beisheim School of Management, Bocconi University, ESADE, and Nanyang Business School.

"Alumni are the only stakeholders you cannot exchange. You might lose students, even dismiss faculty, and ownership might change, but alumni are there for a lifetime," as one dean put it. This means establishing a relationship that endures through good and bad times—a relationship that can be maintained, nurtured, developed, and managed to provide mutual long-term benefits. Accordingly, alumni relations play a role in every accreditation system. For instance, in EQUIS, it's outlined in criteria 3f of Standard 3 under "Students," which reads:

- Describe the way in which the school maintains and uses contacts with its former students.
- Is there an alumni association?
- How is it used to support the school's strategy, programmes, and students in their career development? How effective is it?
- How does the school support the alumni?
- To what extent do the alumni contribute to the funding of the school?

Alumni are the only stakeholders you cannot exchange. You might lose students, even dismiss faculty, and ownership might change, but alumni are there for a lifetime

Value potentials of symbiotic alumni relations

From a purely theoretical management perspective, school leadership must ensure access to strategic resources in its environment with the help of its stakeholders. The most important resources that alumni can provide schools include:

- Knowledge from the world of practice, crucial for school strategy and programme development.
- Future students through testimonials, support in marketing, and personal contact.
- Social capital like trust and reputation that support the school's brand thanks to successful alumni.
- Company and political networks, which provide value for graduates and fellow alumni in their careers, and also research projects for faculty.
- Lastly, finances; many schools rely predominantly on their alumni base for fundraising activities.

There are reciprocal strategic resources that alumni can draw on thanks to their relationship with their alma mater. These include preferred access to knowledge and international research results, lifelong learning thanks to preferred access to tailormade programmes, academic networks which help them in research-related work, and the prestige and reputation of their alma mater and degrees, which are important success factors in their careers. Successful alumni relations always start with identifying the value proposition for alumni. It is clear that pure transactional values, such as discounts for executive programmes, have limited impact, and emotional values of belonging, being embraced and able to contribute are important ingredients for a long-term relationship.

Two models for organising alumni relations

Important questions must be addressed to develop and leverage this symbiotic relationship. The first is the nature of alumni quality and the type of relation, which can be categorised into two models. The integrated model and the traditional alumni association model:

1. **Integrated Model:** This model involves an alumni relations office integrated into the university administration, often within the marketing department. The alumni relations office deals with the alumni and organises alumni-related events. Graduates become 'members' by signing a declaration with a pledge and agreeing to data confidentiality rules. This model is predominant for example in the US and in Asian countries.
2. **Traditional Alumni Association Model:** In this model, alumni relations are managed by a separate, independent organisation with its own board, membership fees, and dedicated membership services for paying members. Traditional European universities like HSG or ESADE operate on this model.

Both models have their advantages and disadvantages. Most importantly in the association model the share of alumni members is usually around just 30% to 40% compared to 90% for the integrated model, although there are exceptions to this general rule. An advantage of the association model could be the active engagement. The deliberate decision to become a member might lead to a higher proportion of engaged and active members in the association model compared to the integrated model. On the other hand, an advantage of the integrated model is the access to data of graduates, which is often restricted for independent alumni organisations due to data protection laws. Furthermore, in the case of the association model, a working relationship between the alumni board and the university management has to be organised, which can sometimes be complicated due to conflicting interests but can also bring in additional energy and creativity. Some schools like WU Vienna and Bocconi in 2018 deliberately changed from an association model to an integrated model, mainly to increase the share of alumni they could have active relations with.

90%

The share of members in integrated models

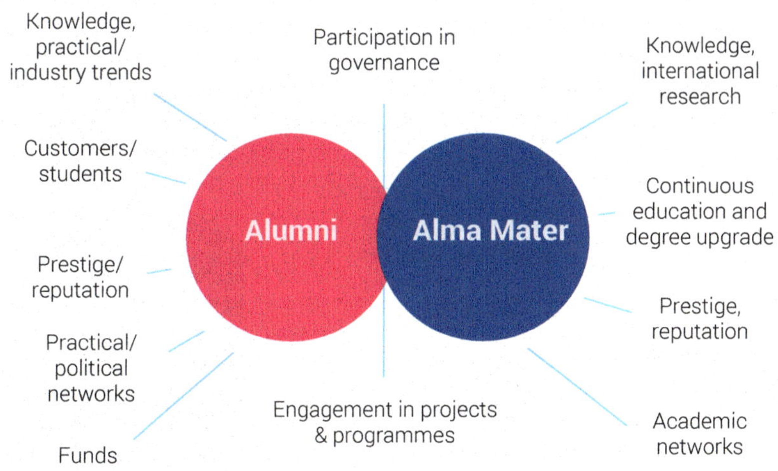

Another important question is how alumni are integrated into university governance. Here again two extremes can be identified. Some schools integrate alumni into their highest decision-making bodies, like the university board, while others establish an alumni advisory board while some only call on alumni on a case-by-case basis, for example for programme development project groups. It seems that a trustful, long-term relationship often requires a form of high-level involvement of alumni, and the alumni advisory board is a kind of a dominant design in this regard. Frustrations which hamper a fruitful alumni-school relationship might occur if too high an expectation for influence and decision rights are not met. Managing alumni expectations, especially regarding involvement in governance, is key.

Success factors in leveraging alumni relations

Alumni engagement takes various forms, including teaching and research involvement. Engagement in teaching includes alumni as speakers in classes, having alumni teaching entire courses, joint development of cases, or real case consultancy projects. On a strategic level alumni provide input in programme development through programme-specific alumni groups. Bringing alumni back to the classroom is a mutually beneficial and motivating experience for both alumni and students.

Engaging alumni in teaching and research projects requires in-depth knowledge about alumni and their backgrounds, making data a crucial component. US-American universities often use elaborate databases that summarise all contact points and contributions. Since these engagements often require direct alumni-faculty contacts, a database on alumni relations by faculty might also help focused engagement.

The key question for all schools is how to maintain contact with graduates in the early career stage

Engagement with alumni is easier for schools located in important economic centres, as they can host events at the school or in their town, attracting a large share of their alumni within close proximity. For international schools, a decentralised system of local chapters is an essential tool, with some schools like Bocconi operating up to 75 of them. Regular contact is a major success factor as it builds trust and familiarity. Some schools therefore set clear goals, such as a minimum of one contact per year.

Role models among leading alumni and their contributions are essential success factors. Career advice is possibly the most important long-term value for alumni. With contribution to careers through networks, career advice, or regular knowledge transfer, the relation to industry or market groups might in the long run become more important than the initial class network, which might be important right after graduation, and maybe again after retirement.

Life journey concept of alumni relations

From an individual alumni perspective, needs, expectations, and the desired level of engagement change over time. A life customer or life journey concept can be an important conceptual framework for alumni management. Key stages include early career right after graduation, the professional phase with family, a potential second career with entrepreneurial engagements, professional reorientations, and finally, retirement. The retirement phase is crucial from a fundraising perspective. Alumni organisations need to define products such as the senior chapter, with a related annual conference in the case of HSG.

The key question for all schools is how to maintain contact with graduates in the early career stage. A phase in life with a high degree of mobility, and thereby changing physical places but also email addresses, the rush hour of life with big and conflicting demands by profession, friends and family. Challenges range from technical issues like database management to being relevant for younger generations, with their new values. Engaging young graduates early on in alumni boards is crucial to addressing their needs.

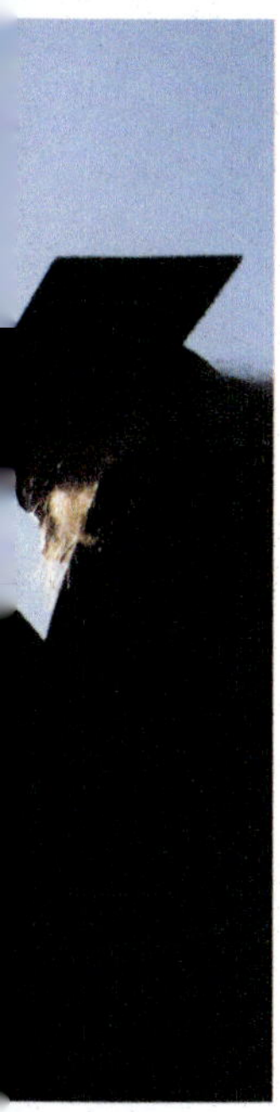

And finally, fundraising

Fundraising cannot be the initial focus of alumni relations, except in emergency cases where schools are short of closure and need immediate help. As one dean put it, if everything is fine and working in alumni relations, then fundraising comes naturally. However, there are important cultural differences. In countries with relatively high tax rates and the expectation that higher education is part of the obligations of the state, building up a fundraising culture is more difficult. The danger that funds raised just serve to finance the reduction of state subsidies has to be mitigated. Iconic, strategically relevant projects might help to create role models for alumni financial contributions like in the case of HSG the new learning centre, SQUARE which was financed by donations of 65 Mio – in an environment of generally excellently funded state universities in Switzerland.

gf

About the Author

Thomas Bieger is Full Professor of Management and Tourism, University of St. Gallen, former President of the University of St. Gallen.

Further information – Conference participants:

Prof. Dr. Markus Rudolf, full Allianz Professor of Finance at WHU – Otto Beisheim School of Management, former President of WHU.

Prof. Dr. Antonella Carù, full Professor of Marketing, Dean for Development and Alumni Relations, Bocconi University.

Prof. Dr. Edeltraud Hanappi-Egger, President University of Economics and Business (WU) Vienna.

Daniel Sánchez, President, ESADE Alumni, Founder Nauta Capital, and former Associate Professor of ESADE.

Prof. Robert E. (Bob) Kennedy, PhD, Dean Emeritus, Nanyang Business School, and Dean Emeritus, Ivey Business School.

Prof. Dr. Bernhard Ehrenzeller, full Professor for Public Law, President University of St. Gallen.

Prof. Dr. Manuel Ammann, full Professor of Finance, President-elect University of St. Gallen.

Dr.iur. et lic.oec HSG Urs Landolf, Tax Counsel Wenger Vieli AG, former President HSG Alumni, Board Member HSG Foundation.

Mathieu Jaus, lic.oec. HSG, President HSG Alumni, Owner Copartner Revision AG.

The Rapid Growth of Hybrid Learning Fueled by the Pandemic

Hybrid learning with simultaneous online and face-to-face delivery is no longer just a response to the COVID-19 disruption but is now a strategic option for business schools. By **Lili Gu**, **Martin Lockett**, and **Yangyang Jiang**

Hybrid learning is increasingly utilised worldwide to enhance learning and provide students with new educational experiences and opportunities. Although not new, it expanded rapidly as a response to the challenges of maintaining educational provision during the COVID-19 pandemic. Hybrid learning is now evolving into a mainstream approach within higher education, especially when learners want flexibility in where and how to learn. Rather than seeing hybrid learning as a second-best or emergency option, it is a strategic option for business schools about which relatively little is understood from both theoretical and practical standpoints.

The initial disruptive effect of COVID-19 was to force educational institutions to go 100% online to ensure the continuity of learning. Then, hybrid learning rapidly formed part of subsequent strategies, as educational institutions sought to provide learning simultaneously to both those who were able to return to campus (or other face-to-face learning locations) and those who were unable or unwilling to return due to travel restrictions and/or personal safety concerns. This dramatically accelerated the adoption of hybrid education, which is now recognised as a sustainable mode of delivery that can enhance the resilience and flexibility of business education.

Learning model	Location	Predominant mode(s)*
Traditional learning	On-Campus	Synchronous
Distance learning	Off-Campus	Asynchronous
Blended learning	On **OR** Off-Campus	Synchronous + Asynchronous
Hybrid learning	On **AND** Off-Campus	Asynchronous

Hybrid learning can be defined as *'simultaneous learning delivery to offline and online audiences'*, which is distinct from blended learning, in which a planned combination of online and offline learning is delivered to a single audience. Online and blended learning have been extensively studied over the past decade. However, while growing rapidly in importance, there has been little research into hybrid learning. Our research and practical experience covers hybrid teaching and learning over a three-year period, based in China. In many ways, China is a 'leading' country in implementing hybrid learning, given that there have been periodic lockdowns in some parts of the country but not others. Also, due to government travel restrictions, international students were unable to travel or return to China for almost three years even when domestic students were almost all on campus.

Our analysis is based on both research and practice. A first qualitative research study was conducted with over 20 teachers engaged in hybrid learning. The purpose was to understand the hybrid learning approach in practice and provide new insights into its benefits and challenges, what influenced its effectiveness and its future potential. A second study, again involving over 20 teachers and leaders, focused on course learning design and institutional support for hybrid learning in a wider range of institutions. The overall approach focused on teachers' perceptions. In-depth interviews were conducted with respondents' perceptions of hybrid learning strategies. In parallel, the authors were all personally engaged in hybrid teaching and one in overall leadership of the school's work. Based on this, the opportunities and challenges of hybrid learning were identified, as well as its potential relevance to future business education.

Benefits of hybrid learning

There was a general view that teachers could not just replicate what they had done previously either face-to-face or virtually. Hybrid learning was seen as a new and different mode of delivery. With a few vocal exceptions, teachers identified a range of potential benefits:

- **Resilience:** During periods of disruption, a hybrid approach catered best to the needs of most students who were expecting face-to-face education, as well as to staff unable to be on campus.
- **Flexibility:** Especially for students not on campus full-time, hybrid learning gives greater accessibility to education and increases the potential reach of education programmes. For example, one teacher saw that, "Institutionally, from a marketing perspective, it allows the university to enrol international students who can't come to the campus."
- **Pedagogical diversity:** The technology-enhanced environment of hybrid learning stimulated a shift in teaching style and pedagogy, bringing virtual technology into education and 'forcing' staff to review their previous pedagogical assumptions and techniques.
- **Educational equity:** Although still different in terms of methods and complexity, it enabled fair treatment of diverse students in the same class at the same time. Moreover, a potential social benefit was that it makes education more accessible to those who cannot afford to attend a fixed study location.

20

A first qualitative research study was conducted with over 20 teachers engaged in hybrid learning.

The challenges of hybrid learning as implemented in practice are substantial and can be categorised into five dimensions:

- **Learner dimension:** Over two-thirds of respondents perceived that online students were mostly silent and were less motivated. Student engagement and offline students recognising the 'presence' of online students were examples of learner challenges. Students had different needs and abilities as well as different physical and social settings.
- **Instructor dimension:** Hybrid learning placed major demands on teachers. 86% saw a lack of management/institutional recognition of the extra work involved, such as the demands in the classroom of managing the different learning experiences of online and offline students as well as dealing with somewhat unreliable technology.

A further benefit during the early stages of the pandemic in 2020 that resulted from the rapid implementation of virtual learning followed by hybrid learning was a dramatic acceleration of faculty members' digital capability. Our school's three-year faculty development plan was achieved in under three months!

Challenges of hybrid learning

Compared with other modes of learning in which students' environments are similar, teachers need to consider the very different environments in which students are located and the need to simultaneously balance both online and offline students. Interaction becomes harder for students, especially those online, and they need to be more motivated. Moreover, the simultaneous implementation of online and offline student interaction becomes more difficult.

- **Curriculum dimension:** Nearly three-quarters of teachers found that even basic forms of interactivity were difficult to maintain when attempting to engage both online and in-person students in a similar way. The lack of an explicit hybrid pedagogy was also a concern. In our university, the focus of staff training was almost exclusively on technology mechanics rather than pedagogy.
- **Technology dimension (controllable):** As most classroom types of equipment were not designed for hybrid learning, 77% of respondents said that there was a lack of fit between classroom technology and hybrid learning. Two-thirds of respondents mentioned that even when familiar with the technology used, they still had technical problems during its operation.
- **Environment dimension (unpreventable or unpredictable):** It was hard to guarantee that the internet environment was always 'up'. When international students were in countries where the network was unstable, issues could not be controlled or resolved by the university. More than half of teachers saw that such technical failures could happen for apparently 'no reason'.

For institutions, management systems developed for traditional education may not be effective for hybrid learning. Expecting teachers to set up a hybrid learning environment in a 10-minute break between scheduled sessions was often insufficient and meant that teachers focused on technical issues rather than on the content of the class. Comparable assessments of the learning outcomes of both online and offline students can be problematic unless well thought-out for fairness and effectiveness, for example shifting presentations to video.

For institutions, management systems developed for traditional education may not be effective for hybrid learning

Overall, without new approaches and support, the demands on teachers are significantly increased in both learning design and educational delivery in ways that can lead to a worse experience for both online and offline students compared with distance learning and traditional learning.

Strategic options for business schools

Our research and experience shows the potential of hybrid learning to drive forward both access and flexibility for learners, as well as resilience to disruption. Given the lack of conceptual clarity around the difference between blended and hybrid learning, confused policies and practices may be adopted that make incorrect assumptions about the nature of hybrid learning. It also shows the danger of managing hybrid learning as a technology

add-on to existing learning approaches. Institutions, therefore, need to make strategic choices about whether hybrid learning is: (1) a stop-gap measure to maintain access in a pandemic in which case quality is a secondary issue, or (2) a new form of learning delivery distinct from distance and blended learning that requires rethinking of pedagogy and the learning environment to be successful.

In our view, hybrid models become most valuable when they are used to create access to new groups of students who cannot always attend in person and want flexibility to arrange their time. Examples are part-time students with variable working patterns, students on internships and those who do not want or cannot afford full-time on-campus study. Whether or not to offer hybrid options and for which courses is an important strategic decision.

Making hybrid learning a success will require resources and management time as well as teaching delivery models with improved staff support and sufficient resources. It will require development of a pedagogy of hybrid learning based on the experiences of teachers and students. Design of physical and virtual environments for the different needs of hybrid learning will also be challenging as it is not an 'add-on' to either face-to-face or online learning. But despite these challenges, hybrid learning can offer new opportunities to enhance business school education and be a positive side-effect of the COVID-19 pandemic!

gf

About the Authors

Lili Gu is a doctoral student researching hybrid learning at Nottingham University Business School China.

Martin Lockett is Professor in Strategic Management and former Dean of Nottingham University Business School China.

Yangyang Jiang is Associate Professor in Marketing at Nottingham University Business School China.

Reshaping Business Education with Hands-On Artificial Intelligence

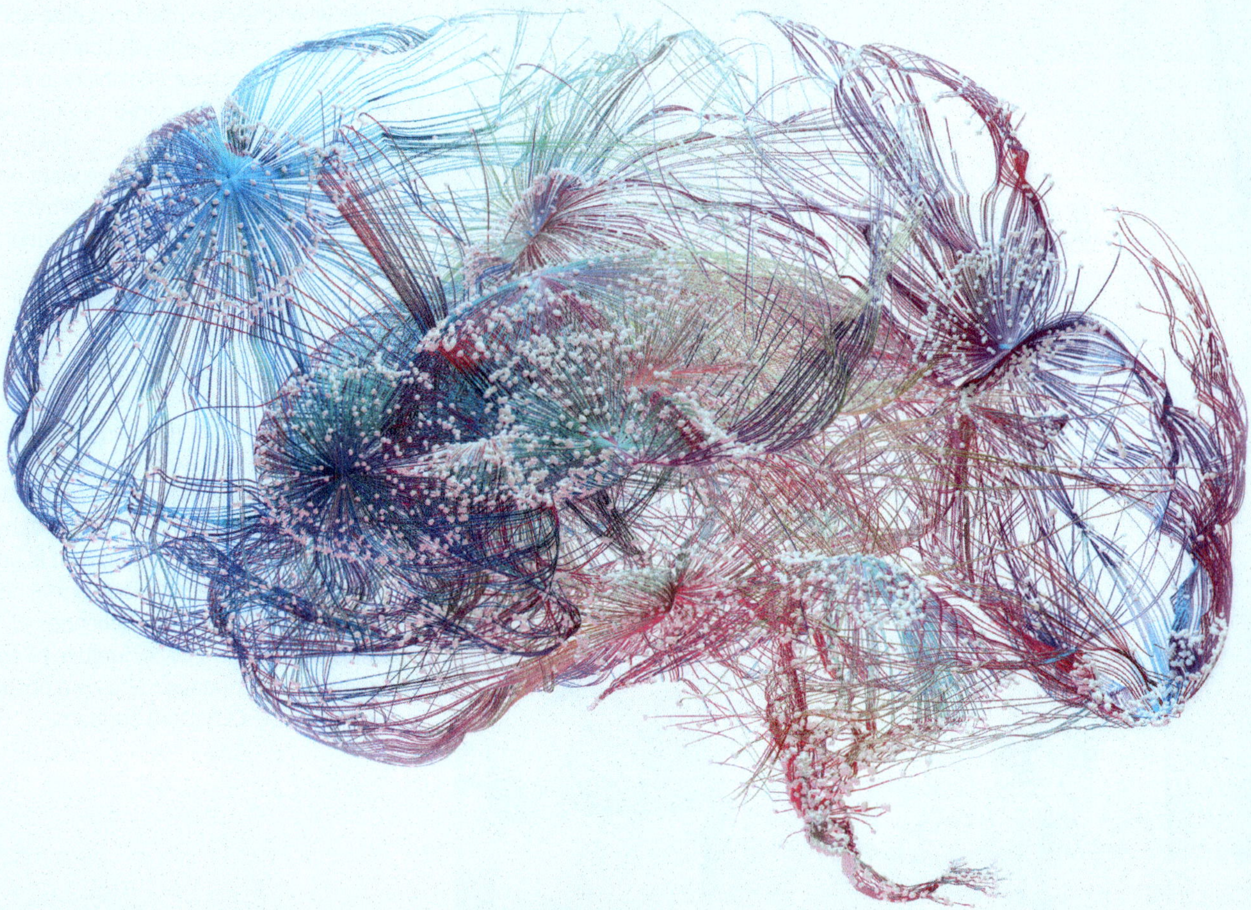

Ana Freire suggests ways of integrating AI into the business school curriculum, giving students an understanding of its potential as well as its limitations

The future of business is being rapidly reshaped by artificial intelligence (AI) and big data, with the World Economic Forum's Future of Jobs Survey 2023 revealing that for companies of various scales, AI and big data are the pillars of corporate training and operational strategy for the coming years. The same report states that approximately 75% of the surveyed companies plan to adopt AI technologies, and this widespread adoption is predicted to lead to a significant churn, signaling a transformative period in the workforce.

This issue places an imperative on business schools, traditionally seen as important centres for advanced education: they must transition from their classic focus on business administration, accounting, and management to integrate cutting-edge technological education that aligns with industry demands.

The question then arises: how can these institutions prepare their students for a world where AI and big data are not just tools but the bedrock of business strategy?

Incorporating AI and big data into the educational landscape requires a multi-dimensional approach:

1. **Enriching current curricula with AI applications:** enhance existing or traditional programmes with specific AI courses tailored to real-world applications and case studies.
2. **Launching specialised programmes:** implement dedicated programmes in data analytics and artificial intelligence, which have increasingly featured in business schools during recent years.
3. **Creating networks and partnerships among business schools:** establish networks for business schools to ensure that, if one school lacks technological courses, it can partner with another that offers such content (even extracurricular), allowing students to acquire the necessary knowledge.

Let's focus on the first strategy, as it presents a practical pathway to immediate curriculum enhancement. Introducing AI through the case study method, especially in established programmes like MBAs, allows students to analyse real-world scenarios where AI solutions are implemented. This approach can demystify AI and reveal its tangible applications across different business functions such as marketing, logistics, and more. Time to be hands-on!

AI in practice: a deep dive into MBA and specialised Master's programmes

We will focus on four common programmes within business schools, discussing practical approaches to integrating AI education:

- **Master's programme related to Business Administration:** Introducing AI into an MBA curriculum should commence with a comprehensive overview of the field - its history, evolution, and current state. This foundational knowledge anchors the subsequent: more intricate exploration of AI systems like robotics, natural language processing, speech recognition, and machine learning. It's crucial for students to understand the breadth and depth of AI, recognising its potential to optimise processes and its implications for the future of work. Through case studies, students can learn to make informed decisions using AI-driven insights. Teaching how AI can aid in talent acquisition, employee retention, performance evaluation, and workforce planning can be an essential part of an MBA curriculum. Do not dismiss the opportunity to teach MBA students basic Python data analysis, not only fostering AI literacy, but allowing them to tap into the full potential of this programming language. This way, students will also be aware of the complexity behind these systems, and this might help when considering their use. Platforms like Kaggle can help to find manageable data sets for basic data analysis and visualisation.

- **Master's programme related to Marketing:** a deep dive into machine learning could demonstrate how AI facilitates more granular customer segmentation and predictive modeling, ultimately leading to more targeted and efficient marketing strategies. Here, practical application is key. Students should get their hands dirty with actual data sets, perhaps using Python, and engaging with Kaggle or GitHub to solve real business problems. Generative AI should also be presented in detail in these programmes, due to the high potential it offers, especially for content creation or personalised advertisement.
- **Master's programme related to Public Administrations:** the focus could shift to AI's societal impact, such as the perpetuation of bias and the essential practices for developing fair and equitable AI systems. If students learn the mechanics of how machine learning models are trained and evaluated, they will gain a clearer understanding of the origins of biased outcomes. Furthermore, computational techniques for bias detection and mitigation need to be explained so students are equipped with the necessary competencies to outline precise requirements for data scientists involved in developing AI applications within the public sector. Finally, these students need to struggle with case studies that expose the ethical and legal challenges posed by AI and learn to craft policies that mitigate these issues.
- **Master's programme related to Sustainability Management:** would approach AI from another angle, showcasing, for instance, how machine learning models can optimise supply chains for reduced carbon footprints and enhanced efficiency. This would not only involve understanding AI's capabilities but also its limitations, such as the inherent carbon footprint of the AI models in order to select the most suitable one depending on the case use. It's key to emphasise the importance of human oversight in deploying AI solutions for sustainable outcomes. The previously mentioned tools (Python and public data and code repositories) can also be useful in this context.

Across all programmes, the instruction must underscore the foundations and the ethical dimensions of AI. As future business leaders, students must learn to pursue AI ethics, ensuring they can lead the development and deployment of responsible and transparent AI systems. The curriculum should include robust discussions on privacy, accountability, and the societal impact of AI, preparing students to make decisions that honour both business objectives and ethical considerations.

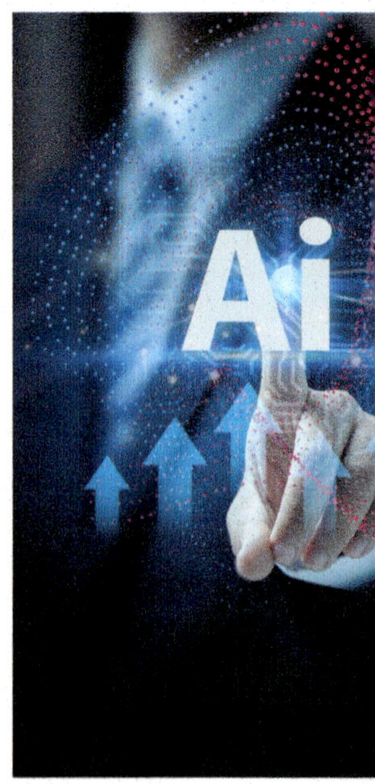

Teaching AI in a business school environment presents several challenges that institutions must face

In each instance, the objective is to move beyond the theoretical and into the realm of application. Business schools have the opportunity - and responsibility - to not only inform their students about AI but to immerse them in the technological, ethical, and practical realities of its use in the business world. This practical approach doesn't just teach students how to use AI, it challenges them to consider its broader implications, making them better prepared for the complex decision-making required in the business world.

However, teaching AI in a business school environment presents several challenges that institutions must face to provide effective education. AI education often needs smaller class sizes to effectively manage and address the individual technical challenges students may encounter, especially when dealing with complex software and coding issues. Unlike traditional masterclass formats that can accommodate larger groups, AI education frequently requires a more hands-on, tutorial-style approach. Business schools must find a balance between providing personalised attention to students' technical issues and the logistical constraints of maintaining smaller class sizes. This demand can put a strain on resources, as more faculty members or teaching assistants may be necessary. This leads to another big challenge: finding faculty with the necessary expertise in AI and its business applications, due to the high employment rates and competitive salaries offered in the tech industry. Besides, instructors not only need to understand AI technology but also how to apply it strategically within various business domains.

Business schools are key to creating multidisciplinary talent: individuals who are not only technologically astute but also aware of the scope and boundaries of current technological progress. By embedding a cross-disciplinary approach within their curricula, these institutions can ensure their graduates have a solid grasp of the possibilities that AI presents, as well as its limitations. This balanced understanding is essential for the next wave of leaders who will drive innovation while remaining conscientious of technology's realistic impacts.

About the Author

Ana Freire is Vice-dean of Social Impact and Academic Innovation at UPF Barcelona School of Management, and PhD in Computer Science.

Embracing Transformation: A Call to Action for Business Schools Around the World

Leon Laulusa looks at how business schools can respond and adapt to social, environmental and technological challenges and help to shape tomorrow's leaders

PICTURE COURTESY OF DAN TSANTILIS

At the start of 2023, headlines around the world were dominated by a new lexicon. Generative AI, ChatGPT, Large Language Models. OpenAI became a household name. In just two months after its launch, ChatGPT reached 100 million users. For comparison, it had taken TikTok around nine months to do the same. The ultra-advancement of technology left every industry astonished and promised to reshape the way we live, learn, and work at a speed that was previously unimaginable.

Today, we stand at the crossroads of a rapidly changing landscape. We find ourselves confronted by not one, but three major transformations: environmental, technological, and societal. These transformations are reshaping the way we interact with the world around us. In this new era, the role of business schools takes on renewed significance. We are not simply observers of change but actors of it. Our duty is not just to adapt but to lead, to initiate and propose new ways of thinking and to equip the next generation of accountable leaders with the tools and mindset they need to navigate these shifting tides.

Throughout ESCP's over two-hundred-year history, the school has traversed revolutions, technological breakthroughs and social upheavals. We have transformed time and time again to ensure the relevance of business education and prepare purpose-driven leaders for tomorrow. And we must do so once again.

In this article, I delve into the pivotal role that business schools play in responding to and supporting these transformative forces, with a specific focus on our commitment at ESCP to driving change in the realms of sustainability, technological innovation, and societal inclusion.

The Environmental Transformation

The urgency of the climate crisis has spurred an environmental transformation that requires a total rethink of business and education. Our model of education and business development has been based on the idea that the sky's the limit when it comes to human progress. In this context, we sought to control our environment at all costs.

Today, we need a new way of looking at the world that ensures harmony with our natural environment and biodiversity. With over 800 million jobs vulnerable to climate extremes and the impact of net zero ambitions according to Deloitte, our future depends on it.

At ESCP, we believe this can be achieved through a holistic approach that integrates sustainable thinking into every course while providing a laboratory for research and practical application to experiment with new business models. In 2021, we established a dedicated interdisciplinary sustainability department to oversee this approach.

Thanks to their efforts, all courses at ESCP now have a mandatory sustainability element. To ensure that our faculty and staff have the foundations of a sustainable mindset, ESCP provides regular training via the Climate Fresk and free, asynchronous online classes provided by Axa Climate School.

Beyond our academic walls, ESCP is dedicated to accompanying learners and businesses in transforming the way they see the world. For example, transforming Africa for a sustainable future by developing its human capital is a prerequisite for an ecological transition. This theme is at the heart of the concerns of our Chair for Responsible Innovation in Africa co-directed by Professors Nathalie Prime and Caroline Verzat. With the platform Commons for Future, ESCP provides open access to all content from the second-year Master in Management course Energy, Business, Climate & Geopolitics run in collaboration with the Carbone 4 Academy. The new STAR (Sustainability Transformation & Applied Research) Centre located on our Berlin campus will be a hub for research transfer, new learning approaches and community building to spark sustainable innovation and new business models.

In the words of STAR Centre co-founder Prof. Florian Lüdeke-Freund: "Sustainability is not a tool to solve business challenges. Business is the tool to solve sustainability challenges." This perspective underscores the vital role business schools play in meeting the challenges (and opportunities) of the environmental transformation. To face this emergency, we will launch accelerator projects on sustainable and regenerative business models.

ABCD

It is our role to help our students to learn about the light side (positive aspects) of the ABCD transformation

PICTURE COURTESY OF DAN TSANTILIS

The Technological Transformation

In today's fast-paced digital age, technological advancement is at the forefront of global progress. The ABCD transformation—comprising Artificial Intelligence (AI), Big Data/Blockchain, Cloud Computing, Cybersecurity, and Digitalisation—is reshaping industries, economies, and societies worldwide. Business schools must look beyond classic management studies to equip our students with the technical know-how to navigate this complex landscape. These skills are not just essential for personal and professional growth but also for understanding the profound impact technology wields on our world.

From our Master of Science in Big Data and Business Analytics to the introduction of 'no code' courses, we are designing programmes to bridge the digital divide and empower individuals from diverse backgrounds to engage confidently with technology. All business school graduates today must possess the digital literacy required for success in the modern business landscape. Democratising access to technology and fostering inclusivity are key steps to ensuring that the technological transformation benefits the greatest number.

While this transformation is technological, true innovation will come if we can combine disciplines. This is something that ESCP Professor of Entrepreneurship Sylvain Bureau discovered over a decade ago with the creation of the Art Thinking method. Invented in 2011, this method draws from observing similar patterns in all types of creative activities, whether in art, science or entrepreneurship, 'to create the improbable with certainty'. By infusing artistic principles into business thinking, we cultivate a new generation of leaders capable of driving innovation and pushing the boundaries of technological advancement.

Ultimately, it is only by embracing technology's potential while addressing its challenges that we can harness its transformative power to build a better future for all. It is our role to help our students to learn about the light side (positive aspects) of the ABCD transformation and to anticipate and prevent their dark side (potential negative consequences).

PICTURE COURTESY OF DAN TSANTILIS

The Societal Transformation

It is now commonly understood that companies that prioritise inclusion and diversity reap numerous benefits. Inclusive workplaces can call upon a broad spectrum of perspectives, experiences and talents to boost innovation, creativity and resilience. Encouraging employees to embrace their true selves not only cultivates a workplace that boosts employee satisfaction and self-fulfilment but also equips them to more effectively meet the demands of an ever-expanding and diverse customer base.

We cannot rest on our laurels or the "old ways" of business if we want to ensure that our students and our societies have a prosperous and resilient future

Businesses and business schools alike must embrace the transformative power of inclusive leadership. At ESCP, our multi-campus model not only enriches our students' experiences but also helps them learn to bridge divides and create connections across cultures and sectors. We've developed bespoke programmes and research initiatives to delve deep into the nuances of inclusive leadership, aiming to empower current and future business leaders to become role models in the workplace. Our Women in Leadership and LGBT+ Leadership programmes do exactly that while helping our participants reach their full potential.

As we face this societal transformation, there is still much to learn to truly embrace inclusion and diversity. With the launch of our new open chair dedicated to Women in Finance, our mission is to understand the causes of underrepresented women in key positions in financial sectors and to bring recommendations for improvements. At ESCP's Excellence Centre for Intercultural Management, Diversity and Inclusion, our goal is to deepen the understanding of intercultural management, diversity, and inclusion-related issues in organisations and to translate the latest scientific insights into practice.

Above all, we have a responsibility, through teaching, student experiences, research and executive education to empower empathetic, adaptable, and effective leaders who can navigate this societal transformation.

Embracing transformation to ensure the future of business (education)

The environmental, technological and societal transformations we face are not separate events. They are not the concern of only one group, region or government. These transformations cross boundaries and are impacting, and will increasingly, impact all of us. As business schools, we have a responsibility to be an active participant in this time of transformation and initiate the new pathway for a better future and society. We cannot rest on our laurels or the "old ways" of business if we want to ensure that our students and our societies have a prosperous and resilient future. The last several decades, if not the last year, have made that clear.

Sustainable thinking, technical acumen and inclusive leadership are the skills of leaders who will face these transformations and change our world for the better. Business schools across the globe have the opportunity to be not just observers of change but actors of transformation. Through education, research and partnerships, we must shape the leaders who will navigate and contribute positively to these transformations. Will we answer this call to action? Our reply is yes.

About the Author

Leon Laulusa is Executive President & Dean of ESCP Business School.

"Have Impact, You Will!" Turning Higher Ed Instructors into Jedi Masters of Sustainability Teaching

The Sulitest team looks at the importance of having eco-literate faculty and instructors to raise awareness and embed sustainability within the student experience

Without the deep and rapid reform of higher education, students today - at best - will be ill-prepared to meet the great challenges humanity faces. At worst, they'll risk accelerating the pace towards disaster.

Episode IV — A New Introduction

In the face of our Earth crisis, many writers have highlighted the importance of changing both curricular design and pedagogical practice within institutions of higher education (HEIs). And changes are indeed being made here and there. But what is happening is more a process of slow *evolution* rather than *revolution*, when what is needed is urgent action. To this end, this brief article reviews how HEIs - in the face of the Earth crisis - respond to the call for curricular reform. In addition, we provide helpful hints on the types of educators who help or hinder you in your efforts to spark curricular change.

"Feel the Force" — The Preconditions of Jedi Power and Action

To answer the question of how we best prepare students to make informed decisions about social and ecological issues, let's first review the preconditions that determine whether an individual student chooses to act for sustainability in the first place.

Research[1] indicates that an individual needs 1) a holistic understanding of the challenges (the 'common language' for all professions) plus a set of knowledge specific to their situation or profession; 2) a range of skills to address challenges at their level (common ones such as system and critical thinking ... and others, more discipline-specific); and 3) the determination to act. The schematic shows that a judicious mix of knowledge, skills, and mindset - what UNESCO calls Education for Sustainable Development - constitutes the seed of behavioural action and the foundation of sustainability literacy that all HEIs need to foster via curricular reform.

Building the Rebel Alliance — The Force Driving HEIs Towards Curricular Revision

A growing number of HEIs are starting to change their curriculum, in response to both ministry directives, and pressures from stakeholders such as students, accreditors, and rankings bodies.[2] For the past decade, we at Sulitest have been working with programme leaders and professors to integrate sustainability more intentionally and more widely into the curriculum. What we observe is that curricular transformation is an iterative process which varies in speed and direction depending on institutional priorities, and the level of engagement from stakeholders, such as instructors, students, administrators, and alumni.

Desired Outcomes of Education for Sustainability

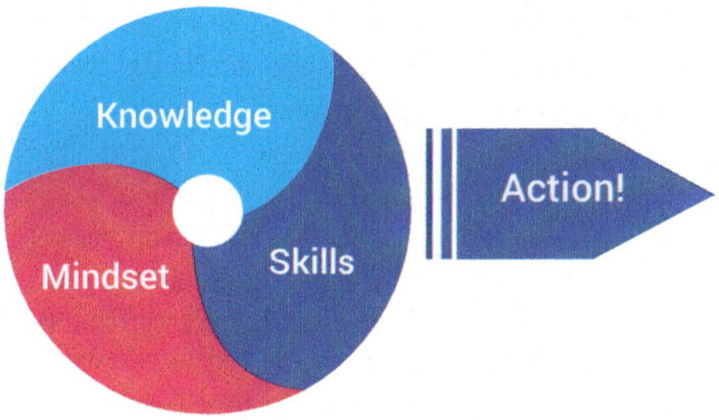

There are multiple ways to raise awareness and embed sustainability learning into the student experience. The easiest step involves organising on-campus events such as conferences, screenings, or thematic activities during a dedicated 'sustainability week' or at the start of a new semester with an inspiring keynote speech or half-day workshops like the 'Climate Fresk', 'The Carbon Literacy Project', or the Sulitest Awareness Test and Quiz. While these actions are more about raising awareness than providing formal education, they have the advantage of reaching large numbers of students, spark an ecological awakening and give them the climate and wider sustainability understanding they need to thrive in a Volatile, Uncertain, Complex and Ambiguous - VUCA future.

Another more ambitious approach is to create elective courses in sustainability such as 'Sustainable Marketing' or 'Responsible Finance'. Often initiated by 'activist' instructors, such courses respond quickly to the demands of concerned students. However, such courses must attract enough students to be 'viable'. Plus, this approach does not address the need for 'mainstreaming' such learning across all programmes. It too often stands as a temporary 'add-on'.

It is also possible—as is currently the case in France—that the Ministry of Education imposes national requirements for establishing a common knowledge base for students. In the same manner, a university president or programme leader can decide to launch curricular reform as a 'political/ecological' initiative. A common response to implementing such 'top-down' strategies is to add a required course or module on sustainability, often in the form of MOOCs.

When instructors are asked to incorporate sustainability concepts into their courses, many just add a dedicated chapter at the end of a course while making only minimal modifications (if any) to established course content. As such, students are taught 'conventional finance' throughout the year and receive only a short

overview of 'responsible finance' at the end. While simple to implement, this approach is ineffective at best, and self-deceptive at worse because it allows instructors to simply 'check-off the required boxes' by adding keywords to their course syllabi without changing the traditional content. It must be said, however, that this approach — while unsatisfactory — is often a necessary step allowing instructors to gradually introduce topics that are new. Some teacher-researchers have also progressively integrated this concept into the course by starting to invite representatives of partner companies involved in their research chair to present case studies.

We have also received numerous comments from students explaining that in recent years, several 'newly converted' teachers have added an introduction on climate change before starting their course. While this shows undeniable good will, the lack of consultation and coordination between colleagues means that these interventions are repetitive and have little impact.

The most complex and demanding approach is undoubtedly to revisit and rewrite all the learning objectives of a programme and then 'rethink' and redesign all courses from the perspective of sustainability

The most complex and demanding approach is undoubtedly to revisit and rewrite all the learning objectives of a programme and then 'rethink' and redesign all courses from the perspective of sustainability. This is a huge task if done properly because it involves not only working on content but also on pedagogical method. However, such eco-pedagogy, action-based learning - learning by doing, and experiential learning all engage students powerfully via a radically revised set of both learning outcomes and instructional methods.

Finally, we know student experiences matter beyond the classroom. Institutions must create exemplary and visible strategies for sustainability in campus operations, environmental management, and social responsibility.

In the end, however, what's most important is that the impact of curricular revision is something real and measurable.[3] The best strategies include a process for measuring impact, for using data to guide and direct subsequent action, and for ensuring that everyone feels both supported in - and accountable for - having a transformational impact on student learning.

May the Faculty Be with You!

While much of the sustainability knowledge students acquire comes from co-curricular experiences such as internships, service learning, exchanges, student associations, etc., it is clearly the responsibility of instructors to transmit core sustainability knowledge.

This is challenging because educators, while experts in their area of teaching, may lack expertise in other subjects, like environmental sciences or social sciences, not to mention the solution-based leverage points—which are all a part of the agenda of sustainability education.[4] Supporting the faculty with practical tools and training thus becomes a major ambition for any HEI wishing to genuinely equip students with impactful sustainability literacy.

> *While they may be aware of some of the challenges humanity faces, and have changed things in their own lives, they are largely oblivious to the connections with the topics they teach in class*

Like the student population it serves, the faculty is highly heterogeneous in its approach to these subjects in terms of interest, knowledge, expertise, and commitment. Three main profiles can be discerned.[5]

1. **The Obstructionists**
   This group includes both '*Deniers*' and '*The Never Wrong*'. The former is apt to claim that the need to address climate change (or other sustainability topics) is exaggerated or less urgent than stated. Because they are often infected by a conspiratorial mindset, there's little hope in engaging them in such curricular review. The latter group - *The Never Wrong* - is hard to reach too, because they are set in their ways and convinced that what they've taught in the past remains just as pertinent for the future. They may represent 10% of the whole population but you can count on both these groups to obstruct - in principle - whatever initiatives or curricular reforms you might propose. Save your energy for other groups.
2. **The Well-Meaning ... but**
   This is a huge group probably comprising about two-thirds of the total. First, we have 'The Disconnected'. While they may be aware of some of the challenges humanity faces, and have changed things in their own lives, they are largely oblivious to the connections with the topics they teach in class. The other group — '*The Disoriented*' - may be aware and troubled by climate change, but they do not know how or where to start. But because this entire group includes the well-meaning hindered only by 'ignorance' or 'lack of training' both these impediments can be overcome. There is a huge opportunity to find allies and supporters across this entire group.

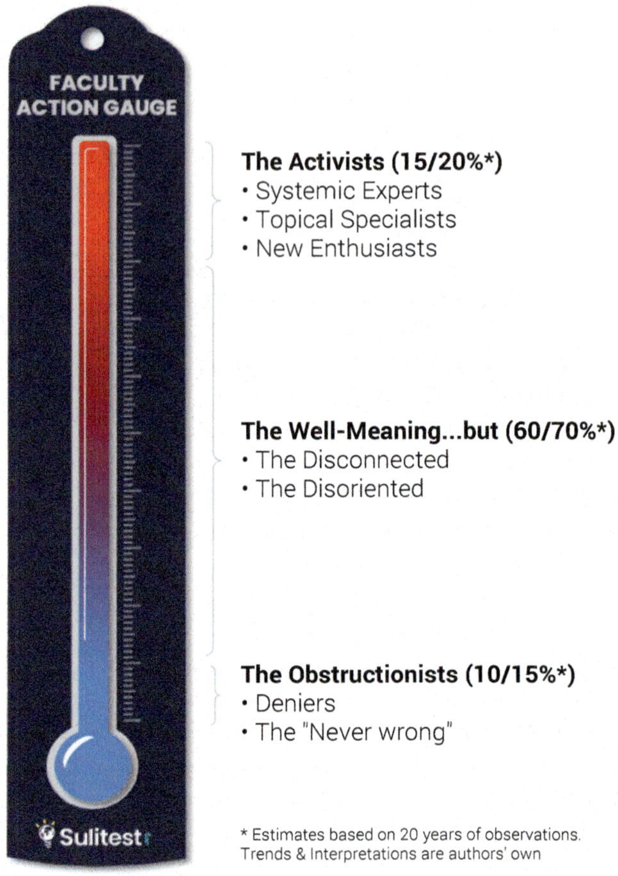

* Estimates based on 20 years of observations. Trends & Interpretations are authors' own

3. **The Activists**
   Three subgroups comprise this group:
   Systemic Experts: Highly qualified and experienced in the field of sustainability, this group has a full understanding of the complex systems underlying environmental, social, and economic issues. Their interdisciplinary approach and holistic vision make them powerful allies in getting diverse instructors connected and committed to the common cause.
   Topical Specialists: This group includes established experts (and probably recognised as such) who have comprehensive expertise on specific topics such as climate change or poverty. They are invaluable as a source of knowledge and training for others when they speak about their own topic. And while they likely lack a systemic understanding of the larger system, it's because they know this that they

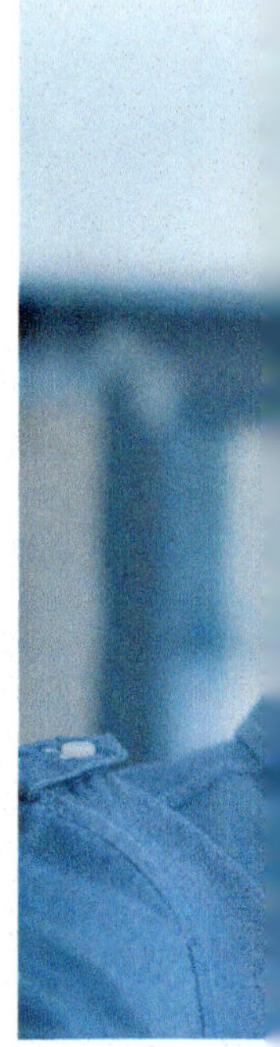

can more easily help others (particularly the *Well-Meaning*) recognise and address curricular knowledge gaps in their courses.

New Enthusiasts: Recently aware and fully dedicated to the cause of curricular reform, this group may - via a 'Dunning-Kruger cognitive bias' - overestimate their ability to embed into the syllabus the appropriate dose of sustainability knowledge. But their energy and enthusiasm for reform is contagious. Use it to help convert the *Well-Meaning* and maybe even some *Obstructionists* in the cause of curricular revision.

Do or Do Not. There is No Try

Given the high stakes of addressing global challenges, it is imperative to engage as many instructors as possible in the curricular review process - whatever their profile. Recruiting new faculty who are eco-literate, unleashing the current faculty already seized by the urgency of the climate crisis, providing support and training to those struggling to keep up, and ignoring those who refuse to budge - these are strategies that work. If higher education is to play its full role in building a livable and desirable future, then this is the new agenda for a new age - changing what we teach and learn in line with planetary boundaries.

A vast undertaking for sure! But how else do we emerge from the dark side! How else do we use our force - The Force - for a new hope?

gf

About the Authors

JC Carteron, Aurelien Decamps, Scott Blair and Estela Pilz are all members of the Sulitest movement.

Footnotes:

1 *Besong, F. and C. Holland (2015). The Dispositions, Abilities and Behaviours (Dab) Framework for Profiling Learners' Sustainability Competencies in Higher Education.* Journal of Teacher Education for Sustainability, 17*(1), pp.5-22*

2 *Read: www.globalfocusmagazine.com/measure-what-is-measurable-and-make-measurable-what-is-not-so/*

3 *https://www.sulitest.org/tools/task*

4 *www.bit.ly/sustainability-knowledge*

5 *This article is based on 20 years of practitioners' observation. The classification and ranges are based on field observations and the interpretation belong to its author.*

Innovate or Stagnate: The New Mantra of Responsible Business Schools

In an era where change is the only constant, can business schools innovate their way to a sustainable future? By **Weng Marc Lim**, **Fara Azmat**, and **Ranjit Voola**

Imagine a world where every budding business leader emerges not just equipped with the standard BBA or MBA arsenal, but also with a vision to reshape our shared future. As our planet grapples with pressing sustainability challenges, business schools find themselves centre stage. Their mandate? Shift from the conventional, and cultivate leaders ready to tackle tomorrow.

Out with the old: why traditional business education no longer suffices

Business landscapes are evolving at a breakneck pace in a volatile, uncertain, complex, and ambiguous (VUCA) world. With this, the hallmarks of top-tier business education are also transforming. The next generation business schools are not simply rehashing traditional teachings centred on profit margins and time-worn strategies - their mission is more profound, more urgent.

Responsible management education (RME) is the cornerstone of this new paradigm. But why such a shift? RME is not just another fleeting trend, it is the clarion call of our times. This holistic paradigm recognises that businesses do not operate in a vacuum, rather, they are part of a larger ecosystem with environmental, social, and economic dimensions. Embracing RME means cultivating leaders who understand the interconnectedness of the world, leaders who are not just business-savvy but also planet-conscious.

Business schools of the future will not just churn out CEOs - they will mould visionaries. These institutions will delve deeper, integrating sustainability not just in lectures but also in hands-on research, innovative ventures, and fostering a new breed of forward-thinking professionals. In this era, success will not be solely defined by balance sheets, but also by the broader impact on society and the planet.

Decoding innovation: beyond the buzz and into the core

Innovation, a term so frequently dropped in conversations that its depth and significance can often become overshadowed, while common to hear, comprehending its true essence requires a deeper dive. In the context of RME, innovation is not a mere accessory - it is the lifeblood. This is not just about birthing new ideas, but rather about cultivating a transformative mindset. One that is not short-sighted, but contemplates the far-reaching implications on our economy, society, and our shared environment.

Damanpour's (1996:694) insight from the late 1990s remains profoundly relevant:

> *"Innovation serves as the evolutionary tool for organisations, either reacting to external stimuli or proactively moulding surroundings, spanning from new products to reinvented organisational structures."*

Innovation in RME is not about fleeting trends or superficial changes. It is about profound shifts in perspective, an unwavering commitment to progress, and the courage to reimagine and reconstruct traditional paradigms. The future of responsible management hinges on how well we grasp and embed this ethos.

> *As our planet grapples with pressing sustainability challenges, business schools find themselves centre stage*

Dissecting the why, where, how, and (so) what of innovation in business schools

Our research led us to a dynamic framework—a blueprint for infusing innovation into business schools. Envision this:

- Why innovate?
- Where should innovation occur?
- How can innovation shape the future?
- (So) what will such innovation look like?

While each business school possesses unique attributes, the essence of 'why', 'where', 'how', and '(so) what' of innovation remains a shared theme. Journey with us as we delve deeper, illuminating each corner of this transformative path, taking examples from our recent works (Azmat *et al.*, 2023a, 2023b).

Drivers of innovation: comprehending the 'why' of business school innovation for RME

Today's business world moves at a whirlwind pace, with myriad forces nudging institutions, especially business schools, to adapt, evolve, and reinvent. We examine these compelling reasons, or drivers, that urge these institutions to innovate, answering the critical question of 'why' such evolution is not just beneficial, but essential.

- **Navigating an uncertain terrain**
  Business schools currently sail stormy seas. The tumultuous environment they operate within demands that they consistently do more, even when resources dwindle. Amidst volatile revenues, there is a pressing need to strike that precarious balance: achieve profitability while ramping up organisational efficacy and output.
- **Bridging the gap with industry**
  The corporate realm echoes with calls for innovation, not just in product or service offerings, but in the very minds they employ. The industry's clarion call? Graduates equipped with a rich tapestry of skills, ready to plug the ever-widening skills gap. Business schools bear the responsibility to reshape curricula and invigorate research, ensuring their graduates are not just employable, but highly sought after.
- **The technological vanguard**
  With the digital revolution upon us, technologies like artificial intelligence (AI), big data, blockchain, and the internet of things (IoT) are not just buzzwords - they are the new normal. This tech tidal wave necessitates innovation in pedagogy and research. Only then can business schools mould students into leaders of tomorrow: agile, relevant, and socially responsible.

The corporate realm echoes with calls for innovation, not just in product or service offerings, but in the very minds they employ

- **Sustainability: the tri-pronged challenge**
  Sustainable development is not a choice—it is a directive. Business schools must address the trio of economic, environmental, and social challenges, pushing the envelope in their teaching methodologies and research initiatives.
- **The accreditation imperative**
  Renowned accreditation bodies, like AACSB, EFMD, and BGA, do not merely value innovation - they demand it. To showcase exemplary standards in teaching, curriculum design, and student engagement, business schools must mirror the ever-evolving trends of the business world, proving their mettle and dedication to excellence.

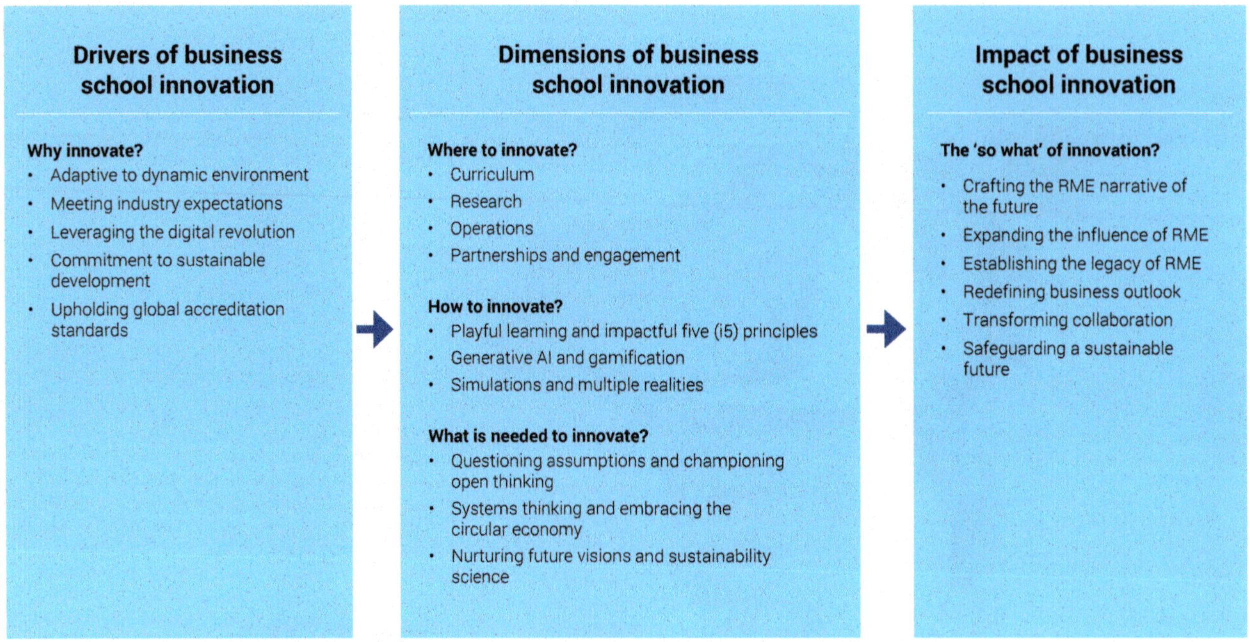

Figure 1. A framework conceptualising innovation in business schools for RME

Dimensions of innovation: charting the 'where', 'how', and 'what' of business school innovation for RME

Innovation weaves itself into a tapestry of dimensions in a business school. As illustrated in Figure 1, we bifurcate these dimensions into two distinct yet intertwined themes: (i) innovation targets, and (ii) innovation as a tool.

- **Bullseye of innovation: innovation targets (where)**
  The 'where' of innovation becomes clearer when we talk about its targets. Think of these targets as the compass points, guiding the trajectory of change within a business school. Given that RME serves as a strategic intra-organisational practice, compelling business schools to weave sustainability threads into their academic fabric, it is imperative to determine which corners of these institutions demand innovative touches. We present a quartet of areas ripe for innovative transformation.

- **Curriculum**
  Today's dynamic business environment demands a curriculum that is not only rigorous but also adaptive, ensuring students grapple with pressing issues like sustainability, ethics, and social responsibility.
- **Research**
  Beyond teaching, a business school's mettle is tested in its research. New methods, topics, and collaborative approaches in research can bridge the gap between academic theories and real-world challenges, echoing the principles of RME.
- **Operations**
  A business school's internal processes - from administration to infrastructural development - should mirror the change it seeks to instil in its students. Sustainable operations can serve as living labs, demonstrating to students the practicality and benefits of responsible management.
- **Partnerships and engagements**
  In a globally connected world, a business school cannot operate in isolation. Collaborations with industries, NGOs, and other educational institutions can amplify the impact of RME, ensuring that the ripple effect of positive change is felt far and wide.

Today's dynamic business environment demands a curriculum that is not only rigorous but also adaptive

Crafting tomorrow's business schools: innovation as a tool (how and what)

In the mosaic of business education, innovation holds the brush, painting vivid strokes of transformation, and on this ever-evolving canvas, we identify two primary aspects: the targets and the tools. We have already addressed the former, now let us delve into the dynamic tools of innovation, exploring both their 'how' and 'what'.

The toolbox: how innovation transforms pedagogy. Innovative tools act as the directors, orchestrating a transformative performance that enriches learning and shapes leaders. Now, let us delve into these pivotal instruments of change:

- **Playful learning and impactful five (i5) principles.** Our current generation faces challenges that are both daunting and multifaceted. Can innovation bring optimism to this landscape? Absolutely. Embracing playful learning not only offers a fresh, positive approach but also fosters liberated thinking and uninhibited ideation. The outcome? Novel solutions to age-old problems. For instance, the PRME's (2023) i5 innovation intertwines playful learning with five pillars - emotional, creative, social, physical, and cognitive skills - cultivating a well-rounded learning experience.
- **Generative AI and gamification.** The digital age bestows upon us the boon of AI, capable of dissecting a vast array of data to glean nuanced insights. Coupled with gamification, which uses interactive experiences to promote sustainable behaviour, these tools possess the power to shape future business magnates.
- **Simulations and multiple realities.** In an era where practical application holds the key, simulations alongside augmented (AR), mixed (MR), and virtual (VR) realities offer immersive, real-world experiences. These tools allow students to grapple with complex challenges, honing their decision-making and critical thinking prowess.

Carving the blueprint: what business schools must do to wield these tools.

To harness the transformative power of these tools, business schools must not only understand their mechanics but also cultivate an environment and mindset primed for innovation. This demands a strategic realignment, focusing on the following pivotal avenues:

- **Questioning assumptions and championing open thinking.** The heart of innovation beats with a yearning to challenge the status quo. The need of the hour? Transition from a predominantly economic-centric mindset to one that values societal and environmental responsibility. Tomorrow's leaders must be adept at questioning deep-rooted business philosophies.
- **Systems thinking and embracing the circular economy.** While individual actions matter, a collective systemic approach amplifies impact. Embracing the circular economy's ethos, business schools should pivot from linear consumption models to holistic, interconnected ones.
- **Nurturing future visions and sustainability science.** Anticipating and shaping the future is integral. Tools like the European Union's Greencomp framework spotlight competencies vital for sustainability, emphasising the importance of envisaging sustainable futures. Collaborative, interdisciplinary approaches are paramount, blending business expertise with broader disciplines to confront multifaceted challenges.

Impacts of innovation: capturing the 'so what' of business school innovation for RME

The traditional business school pillars of commerce and strategy have often faced criticism for overlooking urgent societal and environmental challenges. In today's ever-evolving, obligation-increasing, and stakeholder-driven landscape, it is no longer enough to simply innovate. Instead, the true measure of business school innovation for RME is its tangible, positive impact.

Aligning with global agendas addressing grand challenges such as planetary health and the Sustainable Development Goals (SDGs) is not just a matter of principle - it is a pressing necessity to reclaim the faith and legitimacy that institutions of higher learning command. Ask this: if a curriculum is restructured to emphasise personal climate action, does it genuinely inspire students to change their daily habits? Will a student influenced by such teachings opt for a vegetable-based meal over red meat or prioritise public transportation over a personal car?

Our perspective is optimistic. By infusing pedagogy with novel tools and frameworks aimed at broadening mindsets and enriching skillsets, we are not just creating isolated impacts. Each student transformed by such a curriculum becomes an agent of change. Their individual actions, though seemingly small, create ripples - spurring others, reshaping communities, and gradually, redefining our global approach towards sustainable living and leadership.

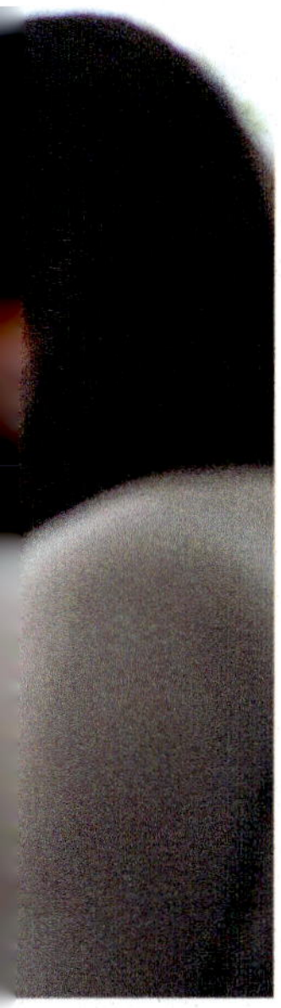

Reimagining business schools: innovation and RME beyond the classroom and into the real world

Throughout history, profound innovation was not just about invention - it paved the way for the narratives of the future. Today, for modern business schools, the narrative of RME transcends traditional teachings, spilling into communities, boardrooms, and global stages, weaving a tapestry of sustainable economics, ethical values, and holistic leadership.

Standing at this juncture, a pivotal question beckons: what legacy will RME craft? If past metrics were revenues and rankings, the touchstones of tomorrow will embody revitalised ecosystems, empowered communities, and the inspired generations championing positive change.

The task ahead for business schools is immense, but the horizon gleaming with opportunities is even vaster. Through a blend of innovative pedagogies, pioneering technologies, and a renewed ethos, RME can sculpt a future where businesses become the embodiment of value-driven entities, championing both profit and principles.

As stewards of RME, our mission surpasses conventional teaching. We are laying the foundation of a future where every graduate is not just a cog in the corporate machine but stands as a guardian of our planet and society.

To every student, educator, business professional, and policymaker, we extend an open call. Embark on this transformative journey of RME with us. Let us not merely envision a brighter, responsible future - let us collaboratively innovate and actualise it.

About the Authors

Weng Marc Lim is the Dean of Sunway Business School at Sunway University, Malaysia, and an Adjunct Professor at Swinburne University of Technology Australia and Sarawak.

Fara Azmat is an Associate Professor and PRME Director of Deakin Business School, Deakin University, Geelong, Australia.

Ranjit Voola is an Associate Professor at The University of Sydney Business School in Sydney, Australia.

References:

Azmat, F., A. Jain and B. Sridharan (2023a) *Responsible management education in business schools: Are we there yet?* Journal of Business Research, 157, *113518*.

Azmat, F., W. M. Lim, A. Moyeen, R. Voola and G. Gupta (2023) *Convergence of business, innovation, and sustainability at the tipping point of the sustainable development goals.* Journal of Business Research, 167, *114170*.

Damanpour, F. (1996) *Organizational complexity and innovation: Developing and testing multiple contingency models.* Management Science, 42*(5) pp.693–716*.

PRME (2023) PRME launches the impactful five (i5) playbook: Transforming business education through creative pedagogies. https://www.unprme.org/news/prme-launches-the-impactful-five-i5-playbook-transforming-business-education-through-creative-pedagogies/

International Student Exchanges: Mobility for Impact

Santiago Garcia and **Gladys Alicia Rey Castellanos** discuss Mobility with Impact, a fundamental shift in the nature of student exchange which will help mitigate some of the environmental costs of student travel and create greater benefits for society

Much has been written on the subject of business schools as agents of change and generators of real positive impact on society. Similarly, much has been argued about the negative externalities of student mobility, accepting that moving students around is a necessary (evil) means if we are to bring the world to our classrooms.

Whereas the general consensus is that business schools must create positive impact and that student mobility comes with an environmental and sustainability price tag, no comprehensive solution has until now been proposed to make sure that such mobility ceases to be seen as a liability, turning it instead into a major actor and generator of wellbeing, sustainability, and positive societal impact.

We want to demonstrate how a business school has transformed this seemingly unsolvable paradox by bringing the classroom to the world, and not just the world to the classroom, while delving on a pedagogical model based on action-oriented learning, Grow by Doing, designed to create impact beyond borders through a new concept of student mobility: Mobility for Impact.

6m

There are roughly 6 million students worldwide moving across countries for their tertiary education according to UNESCO

The environmental costs of student mobility in terms of CO2 emissions could be easily exemplified just by a simple calculation provided by the International Civil Aviation Organization (ICAO). According to the ICAO, a round-trip economy class trip from Amsterdam to San Francisco will have the negative effect of releasing 876 kg. of CO2 into the atmosphere. Much changes for the better when a trip is made within a continent using a more sustainable means of transport such as train, which is estimated to emit 30 to 50 times less CO2 than their equivalent air transport. Whereas intra-European credit-mobility graduates, who could use the train in the context of their exchange programmes, number 390,000 according to the European Union portal Eurostats, there are roughly 6 million students worldwide moving across countries for their tertiary education according to UNESCO. Most of these students, even those moving within a continent for short credit-mobility stays, tend to use air transport when moving across borders (Shields and Lu, 2023).

According to the Higher Education Internationalization Levels Model (Garcia Rodriguez, 2023) the bulk of international activity at educational institutions rests on two types of student mobility: credit-mobility exchanges and degree-seeking mobility. It is essential, therefore, that the sector of higher education finds alternatives to address the growing environmental problem sending or receiving overseas students.

Whereas some small steps and recommendations for educational institutions are being put forward (e.g. Green Erasmus Guidelines for Environmental Activities during Mobility Exchange), we believe that the organisation of bike tours, green marathons, hikes, or promotion of bike mobility within a city are not sufficient measures to compensate the negative externalities of student mobility. Also, it should be our responsibility to make a real difference and impact on the communities where we operate beyond our borders by creating alternatives that generate true and sizable positive impact.

What can educational institutions do, in this context, to make sure the negative effects of student mobility are somehow offset by the creation of positive impact?

We propose that a new concept of student exchanges, 'Mobility for Impact', is one solution that through a multi-prong approach contributes to three goals: pedagogical innovation based on action-oriented learning, sensitisation of students to world problems, and creation of real impact on the host communities.

What is Mobility for Impact and what are the four pillars?

First Pillar: Impact Challenge

Programmes of Mobility for Impact will first identify a key activity in a given area and establish an action plan to provide communities receiving international students with structured assistance in one, or various, of the following areas: Economic, Social, or Environmental Development. This notion of deploying resources to contribute to the societal wellbeing in any of these three key pillars for the development is at the core of Mobility for Impact. Each community, with their different realities and challenges, benefits from the direct intervention of a team of students working together in groups, forming a task force of consultants, with the goal of finding a solution to previously defined economic or business needs, social problems, or environmental issues.

Second Pillar: Structure

Structure is the second defining factor of Mobility for Impact and constitutes the key difference between programmes providing ad hoc stay abroad experiences or awarding academic credit for working at an NGO or completing an internship in an organisation. In this manner, the structured nature of a Mobility for Impact programme implies larger sizes and coordinated cohorts which range typically from 15 to 50 students per semester and destination. In addition, the more permanent nature of the initiatives, which rather than being an ad hoc placement of a student in a project, means ties with the local organisations are established, maintained, and enhanced through long-lasting partnerships that benefit the local community. Usually operating with a local academic partner onsite, the three actors jointly define the different areas of intervention or existing problematics that will lie at the heart of the experience and on which the students will be working with the final goal of providing tangible recommendations, solutions or plans for implementation.

876kg

According to the ICAO, a round-trip economy class trip from Amsterdam to San Francisco will have the negative effect of releasing 876 kg. of CO_2 into the atmosphere

Students reside in the local community where they operate for a minimum of one semester

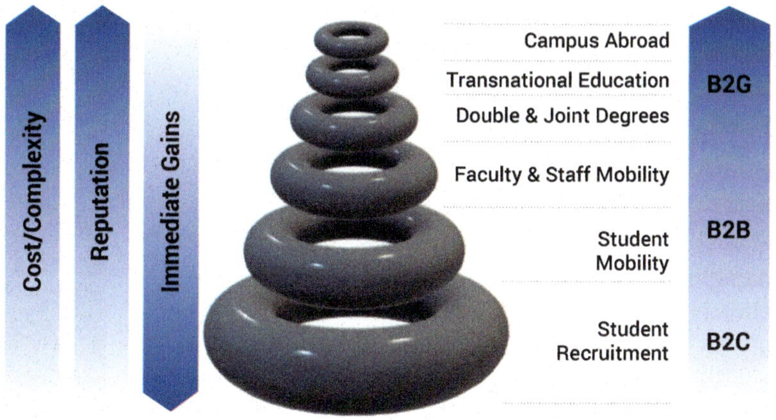

Figure 1. Higher Education Internationalisation Levels Model, Garcia Rodriguez 2023

Third Pillar: Length of Stays.

The third characteristic of Mobility for Impact is length of stays. In Mobility for Impact, students reside in the local community where they operate for a minimum of one semester. This longer duration is in contrast to some shorter-term study abroad (STSA) programmes where students travel to far away destinations for one week to two months of understanding and discovery of different business practices, local realities, economic environments, or cultural immersion. Whereas it is certainly enriching for participants in such STSA programmes (Iskhakova and Bradly, 2021) to become aware of different realities and contrast them with their own, the environmental costs of these activities seem obvious and the general trend and consensus among educational institutions is towards reducing or eliminating such STSA programmes. In contrast, Mobility for Impact initiatives understand the negative externalities of student mobility and try to offset it by lengthening the stays of students in their destinations.

Fourth Pillar: Pedagogical Value

The fourth pillar of Mobility for Impact constitutes the pedagogical structuring of the experience using a 'learning by doing' methodology based on hands-on models such as Experiential Learning (Morris, 2019; Kolb, 1984), Challenge Based Learning (Nichols et al., 2008) or our own educational framework, 'Grow by Doing' in the case of KEDGE Business School. Should we opt to create our own model, this ought to take into consideration the value of the project, the real input of students, appropriate guidance, reflection, and assessment of the experience to ensure real learning while providing maximum impact. In this manner, prior to the hands-on experience, students should be familiarised with cultural, linguistic and subject-specific knowledge of the environment where they will complete their consulting or hands-on project. The guidance by academics and/or practitioners throughout the project aims to ensure students create a tangible deliverable that can be evaluated for academic credit and implemented by the host organisation.

Colombia & Senegal Challenges: Pioneering Experiences

Far from understanding Mobility for Impact as a merely theoretical construct, KEDGE Business School (France) has committed to this type of mobility, aiming to transform first its outgoing student exchanges. To this end, two ongoing projects provide students and the communities they serve with a symbiotic experience of high added learning on one hand, and of real impact on the local milieu on the other.

In this project, a group of 30 to 50 students per semester travel from France to spend one semester in Bucaramanga

The Colombia Challenge, focuses on the economic development of the province of Santander (Colombia). In this project, a group of 30 to 50 students per semester travel from France to spend one semester in Bucaramanga, the capital of Santander province. Once onsite, the cohort follows 6 weeks of intense training on language skills, culture, and legal-economic background to acquaint them with the local environment where they will operate. Thereafter, groups formed by 3-4 foreign plus one domestic student are presented with a real business problem faced by a local company. The tie up with the regional chamber of commerce, the economic promotion agency of Colombia (Procolombia), and the association of business (FENALCO), ensures that the main economic actors of the region are represented and actively

participate in the project. Thereafter, under the guidance of a professor who ensures adherence to and structure of the learning process, students alternate between life at the company and the Business Consulting Center of Universidad Santo Tomás, which acts as the local academic partner. Finally, students present their solutions to the leadership of the company and are assessed by the partner university onsite to evaluate the pedagogical value of the experience.

The Senegal Challenge follows the same structure, though this time students complete one and a half months of courses relevant to their activity abroad and prepare the deployment of a humanitarian project instead of an economic one.

A paradigmatic shift in student mobility is to happen if we are to ensure we want to expand our impact beyond the immediate communities we serve while offsetting the negative consequences of the student journey abroad. The move towards Mobility for Impact may be a key solution to educate, conscientise our future leaders on the multiple challenges the world faces, and provide solutions to current business, societal, and environmental issues while students Grow by Doing.

About the Authors

Santiago Garcia, Ph.D. is Vice President for Strategic Development and International at KEDGE Business School, France and Distinguished Professor at the International School of Economic and Administrative Sciences (EICEA) of the Universidad de La Sabana (Bogotá, Colombia).

Gladys Alicia Rey Castellanos is Director of International Relations at Universidad Santo Tomás, Bucaramanga, Colombia.

References:

Garcia Rodriguez, S. (2023, June 12-14) Sustainability and Impact in Internationalization. *EFMD Annual Conference: The role of business education in an unstable, unpredictable and unsustainable world, Lyon, France.*

Iskhakova, M. and A. Bradly (2021) Short-term study abroad research: A systematic review 2000-2019, Journal of Management Education, 46*(2) pp.1-45.*

Morris, T.H. (2019), Experiential learning: a systematic literature review and revision of Kolbs model, Interactive Learning Environments, 28*(8) pp.1064-1077.*

Kolb, D.A. (1984). Experiential Learning: Experience as the Source of Learning and Development. *Englewood Cliffs: Prentice Hall.*

Nichols, M.H., K. Cator (2008), Challenge Based Learning White Paper. *Cupertino, California: Apple, Inc.*

Shields, R.A., and T. Lu (2023) Uncertain futures: climate change and international student mobility in Europe. Higher Education, 19th April. *https://doi.org/10.1007/s10734-023-01026-8*

It's Time to Treat Business Education Differently

The challenge-driven curriculum at Hult International Business School promotes critical thinking and prepares students for the workplace with real business cases. **Matt Lilley** asks if this could be the future of business education

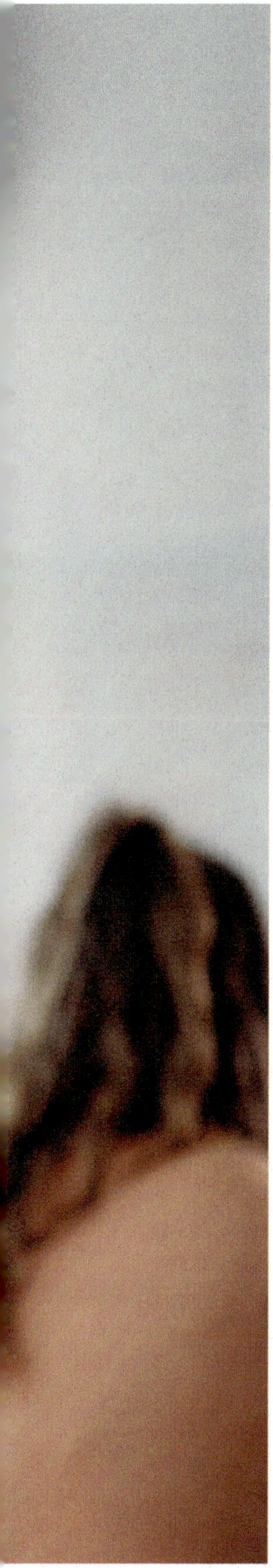

For most people, the decision to go to business school is a practical one. People come to business school to further their careers and to learn new things, in hopes of applying that learning to the business world.

Yet, higher education in general has been centred around research and the pursuit of knowledge, often with little focus on the practical application of these ideas. Does this mean our institutions have been approaching business education the wrong way?

To stay relevant, a business education should incorporate both theoretical and practical elements into its teaching. It is essential that a business school curriculum reflects the real world, particularly as we are educating many of those expected to make a significant impact in the economic and societal issues of the future.

Business students must be exposed to the types of challenges that real companies face on a regular basis and they must learn to solve the tasks they might be expected to complete after graduation.

With this in mind, Hult International Business School has developed a curriculum that approaches business education differently, centred around challenge-based learning that helps students not just understand what is expected in real-world business environments, but also how to put this learning into practice. Here are just a few of the steps Hult has taken to prepare graduates for the future of business:

Solving challenges through a critical lens

With student employability as a core focus, Hult proactively looks at what employers are expecting from business school graduates and brings that perspective back into our classrooms. Furthermore, as game-changing technologies like AI become more powerful, human skills such as critical thinking become increasingly important; and with access to knowledge more widely available, what's becoming more critical is how that knowledge is *applied.*

Critical thinking is taught at Hult International Business School through a business lens. We teach people to work well in teams, and in complex, diverse environments. We want our students to excel at the things only humans can do, not the things AI can do – skills like teamwork, hands-on management, and reacting to unexpected changes in complicated, challenging environments and knowing what questions to ask.

That's why we encourage our students to use AI in their work and show them how it can complement, not replace, the skills they've developed while at Hult.

Hiring faculty who focus on teaching

In many business schools and universities, professors aren't hired on their ability to teach. At Hult, our professors are teachers first, researchers second. We know that research is important and has its place in business and society. We value it greatly and contribute via our Hult Impact Research Labs and through various faculty projects.

But at Hult, we hire individuals who are great teachers first, with a passion for their area of expertise. If business schools are going to ask students to give up a year or so of working and pay us tuition fees, they cannot afford to compromise on teaching excellence. We provide this at Hult. It's our job as educators to develop the essential skills required to be successful and bring about change.

We bring together forward-thinking people from all over the world to learn business by doing business. Through our teaching, Hult students become highly employable and ready to make an impact on the world.

More than any other discipline, business students must be exposed to real business challenges, working on the types of tasks they might be expected to complete after graduation

Context is as important as content

We believe that context is as important as content. Students need to know why they're learning something. As much as possible, we're trying to simulate a business environment for students while they learn, putting everything into this challenge-based context. We are helping to develop strong leaders and managers - years before they would encounter this type of training via development programmes provided by employers.

As Hult's curriculum is challenge-driven, it is designed as a series of group exercises. We partner with real businesses, who offer our students the opportunity to take part in genuine challenges their organisations are facing. After teaching Hult students the knowledge they need to solve these challenges (whether that is finance, strategy, marketing or other 'subjects'), they'll then work in small groups to apply this knowledge and come up with solutions.

That's why when we recently re-designed our new Bachelor's in Business Administration, we partnered with Burning Glass Technologies to review and learn from some 50,000 job postings. We wanted to capture the key skills and capabilities that employers are recruiting for, all the way from graduate roles to senior management.

We created a skills dashboard to assess the top 30 skills and then worked to embed these into the programme's core. Throughout the programme, students are assessed on the application of skills and mindsets that are essential to a successful career on a global scale and – really importantly – given feedback on how to improve.

We are helping to develop strong leaders and managers - years before they would encounter this type of training via development programmes at commercial companies

Teaching people to structure and communicate their ideas

Learning how to communicate is an important part of the training we offer at Hult. To have an impact in the world, not only do you need to bring new ideas or do great work, you must be able to communicate information in a way that people understand, and that helps them remember and act on. We train individuals to structure their ideas before they speak. We expect students to communicate these ideas in a simple, effective way.

To help with this, when students are set a real business challenge, they'll not only come up with a solution, but present that solution in front of the class. Part of their grades will be based on this presentation.

To complement the challenge-based learning, Hult's career services help students accumulate and present their professional experiences to potential employers. Each student at Hult has a personal career and development coach who works with them to better understand a student's strengths and weaknesses, and to help connect these learnings with specific career goals. We help students decide on the story they want to tell, and to help them to fill the gaps.

This is why 98% of our graduates are employed or in graduate school within six months of graduation.

Diversity in the classroom

Many schools say they are global, but I would argue that none are global in the way that Hult is. We have students and faculty from some 150 nationalities, with no one nationality making up more than 10% of our community in a given school year.

After all, one of the hardest skills that anyone can learn in business and management is how to manage people who are different to you. At Hult we want to teach students how to have those difficult conversations, how to manage people who are different to them and how to receive feedback as well as how to give it.

It was only when I started travelling that I realised how many things I thought about the world were influenced by where I'd grown up, and how other people have completely different ways of thinking.

At Hult, students will be completely immersed in this diverse environment from day one. Everyone is different from each other, and most of the work is done in teams.

Then, of course, there's the alumni community, which is made up of more than 30,000 people, who are working in just about every industry and every country on Earth.

A different approach to business

Students are smart, perceptive, and forward-thinking. They like having the opportunity to work on real projects, debating solutions with their clients.

When I talk to graduates, years after they've left Hult, it is this approach and the skills they've built that they particularly remember about their schooling, not just the knowledge. They remember the teamwork, the problem-solving, and learning to understand different perspectives.

People often ask me, "what will business education look like in the next five years?" I answer that in five years' time, a lot of business schools will look like Hult does today. Challenge-based learning really is the future of business education.

About the Author

Matt Lilley is President at Hult International Business School.

The Role of AI in Corporate Learning

Martin Moehrle discusses how Corporate Learning can embrace AI

Generative artificial intelligence has taken the world by storm. It attracts a huge amount of venture capital and pushes up the market valuation of any organisation connected with AI. The current hype also raises questions about its long-term impacts on the world of work. There are a lot of projections out there, from dystopian to utopian, that all anticipate enormous change. Hence, we would like to explore here the role of Corporate Learning in facilitating AI-driven corporate and workforce transformation.

As depicted in Figure 1 (page 70), we see two forces at play in today's corporate world, rooted in both the industrial as well as the post-industrial era. In the industrial context of the 20th century with clearly defined repetitive processes, robots and algorithms will increasingly perform tasks that were previously accomplished by humans. In the knowledge era of the 21st century, humans will augment their intelligence and propel their productivity with the help of AI. This could lead, in the remainder of this decade, to significant gains in labour productivity. However, only under the condition of a highly adaptable labour market with flexibility on behalf of all stakeholders: governments, employers, unions, workers, and the education sector.

As with any new technology, some observers focus on the risks, whereas others emphasise the opportunities. We must decide if we declare AI as our friend, being aware of the inherent risks, or if we try to ban it as our enemy. Only a critical-constructive approach will allow us to realise the underlying potential of AI technology i.e., we must allow for experimentation, whilst monitoring outcomes to inform regulation.

Corporate Learning should, in our view, address four action areas (see Figure 2):

Firstly, AI can significantly improve the efficiency and effectiveness of learning practices and the learner experience. It is a must do for L&D to keep their own function competitive.

However, learning functions must look beyond their immediate remit to remain an integral part of value creation and hence, embrace the following other three areas:

Secondly, with AI transformation, repetitive tasks will get automated, provoking a significant demand for up- and reskilling that Corporate Learning must anticipate and manage.

Thirdly, to realise the power of AI to augment knowledge worker productivity and improve user experience, AI literacy must be ramped up across the board.

Lastly, Corporate Learning should contribute to the organisation's deployment of an ethical framework and public discourse on the responsible use of AI.

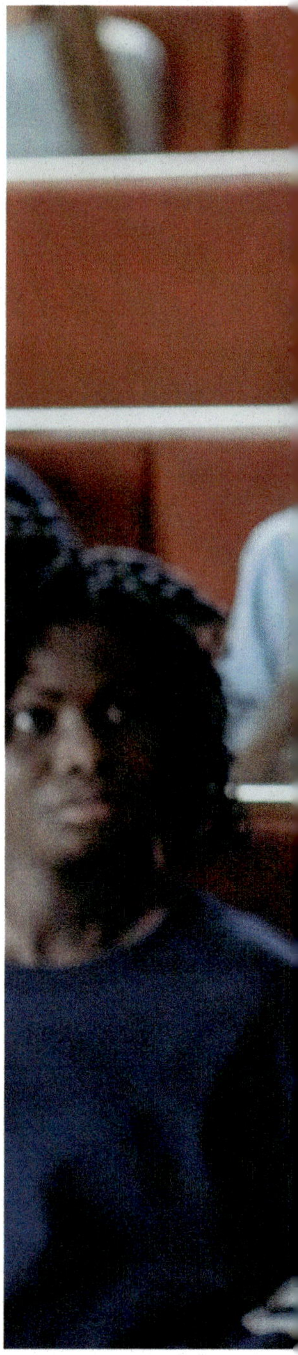

There are a lot of projections out there, from dystopian to utopian, that all anticipate enormous change

AI applications in L&D

When it comes to the many forecasts of AI applications in the Human Resources domain, learning and development is regularly put in the front seat.

EFMD and HEC Paris recently teamed up to run a workshop for L&D executives with the provocative title *Will AI give us superpowers, or will it replace us?* Among others, four companies presented an AI use case. Forvia's use of an AI powered recruiting tool has significantly increased efficiency and effectiveness of its talent acquisition practice, leading it to now explore its use in internal staffing and mobility. dsm firmenich trained its learning community in using Chat GPT to develop personalised learning journeys for specific skills, and for them to then teach the broader workforce. Intercorp Group can now consider any feedback from learners in refreshing its programmes and sharply reduce the time designing learning programmes, by using a variety of AI tools, including Chat GPT. And Schneider Electric shared their use of AI to support new habit adoption through nudging e.g., in their efforts to empower women to rise into managerial ranks.

An ever-increasing number of published use cases show that AI can be a game changer along the entire learning value chain. Future skills and respective learning needs can be anticipated early on. The more skills databases are properly populated with quality data, the better.

The design of learning programmes and learning journeys can be accelerated dramatically, down to a very personalised level. When using a learning experience platform with many digital learning assets, curated by L&D, AI can fully personalise the learning environment, given a person's role, peer group, current and desired future skills and learning preferences. Chatbots can provide instant support and improve learner experience. With increased digitalisation, AI can seek learner feedback and monitor learner activity which again should drive the impact of learning.

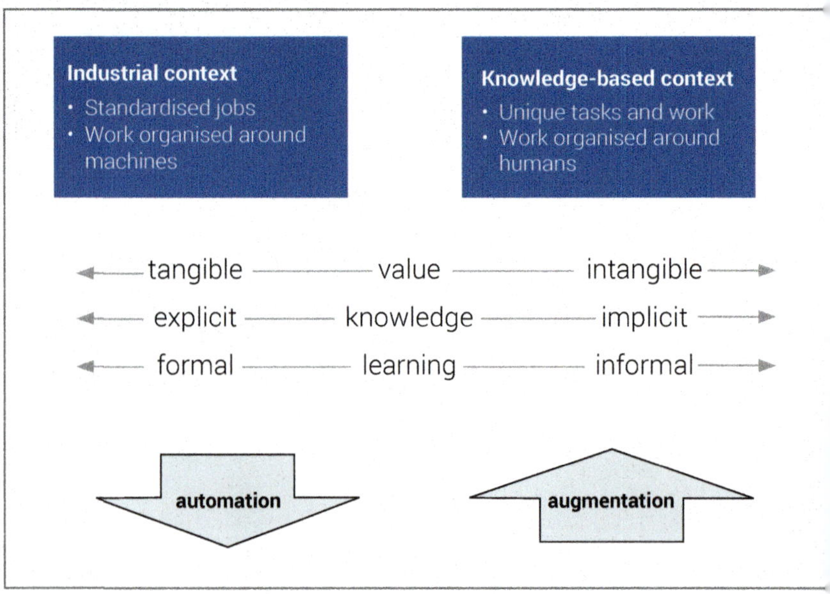

Figure 1. The impact of AI on workforce productivity

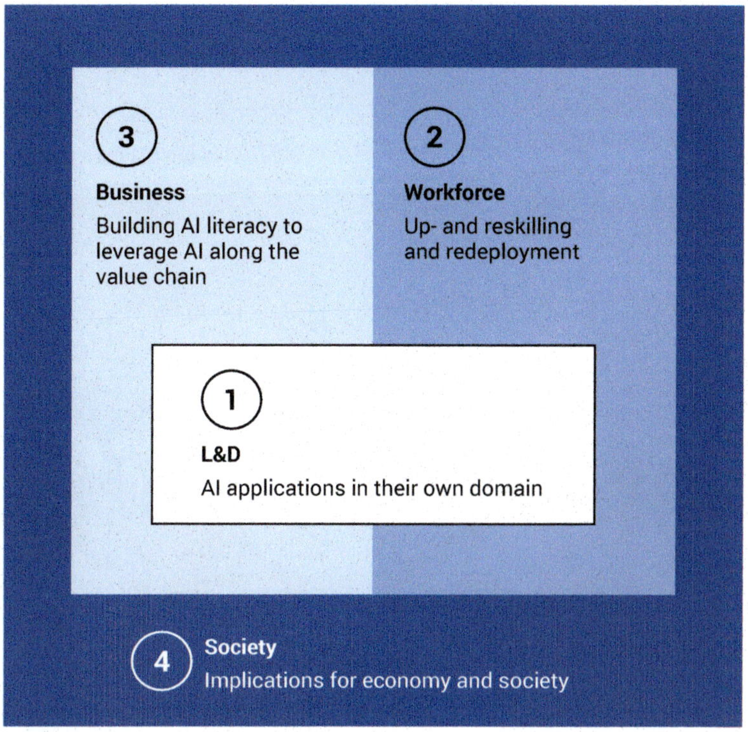

Figure 2. The four action areas of AI in Corporate Learning

The opportunity space for AI applications is similarly large when it comes to assessment, performance management, DEI, succession management, talent analytics, engagement, wellness, etc. It is high time for learning leaders to invest time and provide opportunity for their teams to experiment with, and build confidence in, the proper use of generative AI tools such as OpenAI's Chat GPT, or Google's Bard, or Microsoft's Bing, in addition to using talent-specific AI-powered tools.

Retention of talent will become essential, even when significant investments in up- and reskilling are required

Up- and reskilling

The skills required to complete tasks that get automated will become obsolete. At the same time, humanistic skills (empathy, teamwork, critical thinking, judgement, curiosity, etc.) and digital skills will continue to gain in importance. The ability to co-pilot with AI and augment own's own productivity will become most important. This workforce transformation has been going on for a while but will further accelerate with AI adoption. Skills will become the preferred unit of analysis, thereby complementing, or even replacing jobs as the planning unit in strategic workforce planning.

Unemployment rates are down, and the tight labour markets will become even tighter with the upcoming retirement of the baby boomer generation. Recruitment will not be the solution to acquire new skills alone. Retention of talent will become essential, even when significant investments in up- and reskilling are required. This also positions AI as our friend, and not the 'enemy who kills my job'.

Workers in lower-wage jobs (and women) are much more likely to need a change of occupation. Thus, workforce transformation will also become a social and DEI issue. Corporate Learning must get prepared for this up- and reskilling challenge, through specific learning journeys and badges, part-time degrees and certificates, or talent innovations such as an internal talent marketplace, and dedicated multi-year workforce transformation funds.

AI literacy

Several studies show that HR and L&D are not yet at the AI strategy table which, in our eyes, is a huge mistake: AI transformation is more of a people than a technology challenge.

AI literacy can be systematically developed by self- and peer learning toolkits or by cascading a team-based AI exploration journey throughout the organisation whereby teams are assigned with creating an AI use case, combined with reflecting ethical considerations (more about that below).

Corporate Learning could also run a series of AI workshops in all businesses and functions with the aim to identify automation and augmentation opportunities that could then be aggregated and form the basis of an AI implementation roadmap. The prize is high, and productivity gains of 15% and more are being anticipated.

Most AI tools don't explain how they came to their conclusions, and even the engineers of these tools can't explain

The most obvious areas for AI application, across industries, are customer service and personalised marketing for improved user experience. Recognising patterns and weak signals in huge amounts of data is the other ubiquitous application. And then, any knowledge worker should be able to augment his or her productivity by smart and responsible use of generative AI. A well-orchestrated AI literacy initiative, in combination with an AI roadmap buildup, should be, in many cases, the best approach to realise the potential of AI.

AI ethical framework

AI is highly disputed because it comes with many risks that we need to learn to properly manage. There are privacy concerns about data usage, and cybersecurity finally gains the importance it should have had years ago.

AI tools get trained on as broad a range of data sets as possible. However, these data should represent the desired future state, but often enough, represent only the past. Hence, the tool might provide answers and recommendations that are biased toward past realities.

In addition, most AI tools don't explain how they came to their conclusions, and even the engineers of these tools can't explain. Occasionally, AI tools tend to hallucinate i.e., make things up which are not true.

Therefore, we need to understand the frontier between automation and augmentation. This frontier is dynamic and might allow for more automation in the years to come. However, we should only automate processes where risks are clearly understood and managed.

Organisations are well advised to draft, clearly communicate, and follow through on *Responsible AI Use Policies* that leave the accountability for AI use with the user. Augmentation stands for using a co-pilot for the enhancement of one's capability. Any piece of work that uses AI must be owned by the user, and AI use must be made transparent. The more the use is demystified, the better for its transparency.

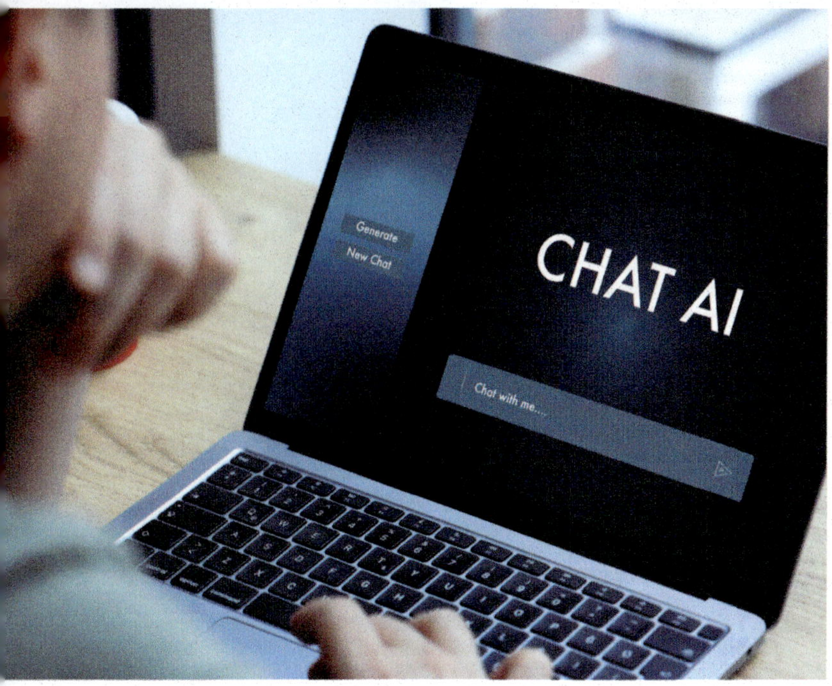

Conclusion

AI is anticipated to clearly accelerate labour productivity, which has been flat for many years, and to enhance user experience. As with any new technology, there are opportunities and risks, and all kinds of fantasies about its impact. Only an AI-literate workforce knowing its limitations and risks, will reap the successful harvest of an AI dividend. And only an organisation that generously facilitates up- and reskilling and expects a responsible use of AI will create a climate where AI is regarded as a friend. This provides Corporate Learning with vast opportunities to facilitate and add value to AI transformations.

gf

About the Author

Dr Martin Moehrle is a Management Consultant and Director of Corporate Services and of CLIP at EFMD.

Demystifying Student Experience

In March 2023 EFMD hosted a Student Experience Workshop, with the theme of 'Creating Value Beyond the Curriculum: Wellbeing and Engagement'. **Stephanie Lambert** reports on the importance and increasing awareness of student wellbeing

How do we create a high quality, positive student experience? That is a major question that affects nearly everyone working in Higher Education. Student wellbeing and engagement can make the difference between an individual being a high-achieving graduate or not completing their studies. Yet, all too often other aspects of education in institutional strategies take precedence.

To tackle the issue head-on, in March 2023 EFMD Professional Development hosted the first in-person iteration of our Student Experience Workshop. The theme was 'Creating Value Beyond the Curriculum: Wellbeing and Engagement'. Over one and a half days, 21 participants representing 13 countries met in Brussels to learn and share aspects of these two key facets of student experience, and the interplay between them.

The term 'student experience' is reductionist to say the least. Not only is the subject matter complex (Where does experience start and end? What does it include? Where does it happen?) but it will manifest differently depending on your viewpoint. In the EFMD Offices we gathered together Programme Managers, Directors of Student Experience, Study Advisers, Student Services Managers, Department Heads, Vice-Deans and even representatives from psychological services, to dissect the issue. Being in the room together created a brilliant opportunity to scrutinise what student experience meant through different lenses. We discussed, in depth, how we could foster purposeful learning journeys for business and management students. Some of the thoughts we had, and the key themes we went over, are captured here.

Learning beyond the classroom

Ultimately the key stakeholders of our institutions are the students themselves, a heterogeneous group representing different backgrounds, learning styles, motivations and desired outcomes. One thing students should have in common is the expectation to learn, develop and to be supported in that journey. As universities we want students to graduate with a meaningful education, ultimately reaching their full potential. Degrees should not only equip students with knowledge, but also with the skills and behavioural competencies to thrive in the workplace or for onward study.

The visions and strategies of business schools focus on creating well-rounded leaders and individuals who aren't only driving organisations to success but are working towards the good of a larger society. Many strategies champion diversity, encourage entrepreneurial confidence and highlight the honest responsibilities of leaders. And there are plenty of business schools that claim to furnish students with the ability to manage their professional and personal lives in a conscientious way too.

Being in the room together created a brilliant opportunity to scrutinise what student experience meant through different lenses

Education can teach this, but these parts of personal development are often nurtured somewhere beyond what we teach as part of the curriculum, and are rooted in other parts of the student experience.

Many of our students will expect support around careers, wellbeing, student living, study skills to name but a few. Student experience can be considered as a sort of tangible return on a large investment in terms of time, effort and finance (especially in contexts such as the UK with increased fees and cost of living). They are often throwing their life and soul into their education and we need to recognise that.

In the wake of the pandemic there has also been a spotlight on the mental health of our students, and questions arising over the level of care that can be expected in educating predominantly young adults. While this problem already, and has always, existed there is thankfully now a heightened awareness around the issue. There is much more open discussion, and action focused on how individuals are treated in regard to race, gender and neurodivergence and many other nuanced parts of lived experiences. The make-up of who each person is as an individual can fundamentally change their lived experience. By recognising people as diverse individuals we can all the better guide them on their path through education.

The shake up to education on a global scale, brought on by COVID-19 drew the spotlight onto the wider student experience. Suddenly lecturers were speaking to a hundred people in their bedrooms, an invasiveness that made it hard to ignore student's lives outside the lecture hall. Students missed out on so much during this period, we have often been scrambling to fill those gaps as they returned to education in person. But it helped us see the importance of that wider student experience, the value of being in a room with others, of socialising on campus, or the serendipitous conversation you might have with your professor.

The extra enrichment of a full student experience creates the comfort and freedom to inspire people to better things.

The bigger picture: where student experience fits in

One of the challenges raised by the participants at our workshop was around where student experience was steered from within institutions. There are a number of players in each establishment in student experience, with competing tools for management and coordination (or lack of) between departments and services. It takes a team that reaches to every part of the campus, who can oversee various aspects and bring focus and unity.

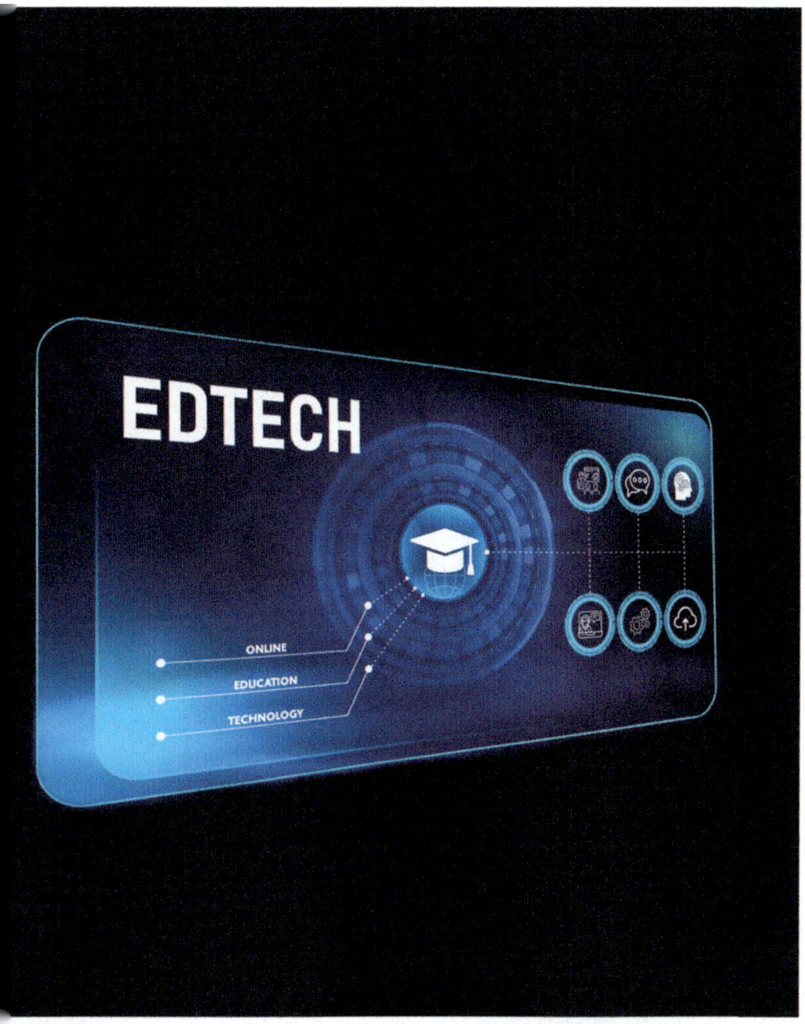

Every institution needs to make decisions over strategic resources

One example discussed at the workshop was the role of IT and data technology services. Allowing the tracking of 'engagement' on learning platforms, logging attendance, student journey mapping tools, and effective administration tools were not only jobs for those in student-facing roles, but ones that needed to be enabled by fit-for-purpose technology. And, of course, the personnel to facilitate the relationship between departments.

There were examples of where a place for improving student experience sat clearly within the curriculum, with some schools offering wellbeing modules for leaders as core or optional credit-bearing parts of their programmes. Not only was this for the benefit of the graduates, but also for a wider societal good in developing leaders that have an awareness of the importance of wellbeing in the workplace.

There were also deeper challenges in the room. Every institution needs to make decisions over strategic resources. Student experience comes at a cost in terms of staffing, finance and time. Whilst roles around student experience can be very rewarding, institutions also need to acknowledge the toll that some types of caring work can take. Participants at the workshop agreed that there needed to be a "transversal awareness of the importance of student care." It can't just be a tick box exercise, it must have deeper roots in our organisations.

> *Teachers and programme directors must consider if certain learning methodologies are relevant*

That transversal awareness helps create added value and can perhaps answer some of those questions about resources. A strong student experience for example, can become part of the marketing arsenal of the institution more broadly. Thinking about the end product too, students who enter the jobs market as resilient individuals with a 'healthy life' approach, is something an institution can be proud of.

The smaller picture: engagement vs attendance

Whilst the larger scale of student experience was covered, there was also a deep dive into the detail. An emergent and unexpected theme from the workshop was understanding the role of engaging students in their learning journey and how they might drive their own student experience, especially in terms of attendance.

Since the pandemic we have seen a shift in how students show up in the lecture halls and classrooms. Faced with rows of open laptops one can't help but question whether the typing is detailed note-taking or alternatively a job application or doom scrolling through social media.

Difficulties lie in encouraging some of our less mature students into the classroom in the first place. And this was a challenge shared by the room, there was a collective relief as each member realised they weren't alone in this. With online lessons and lecture recordings available wherever and whenever, and (for some students) sped up at twice the speed, some students felt they could work smarter – or seemingly with less effort. Some of these behaviours have continued, even where provisions have returned to in-person.

If students aren't attending, then we need to ask why. Does the two-hour lecture add value? Where is it suitable? Teachers and programme directors must consider if certain learning methodologies are relevant, and if they are, then how is this value communicated to students? We agreed that attendance is not engagement, but it certainly holds weight in whether a student completes their studies, and the opportunities that they can open up for themselves by being present.

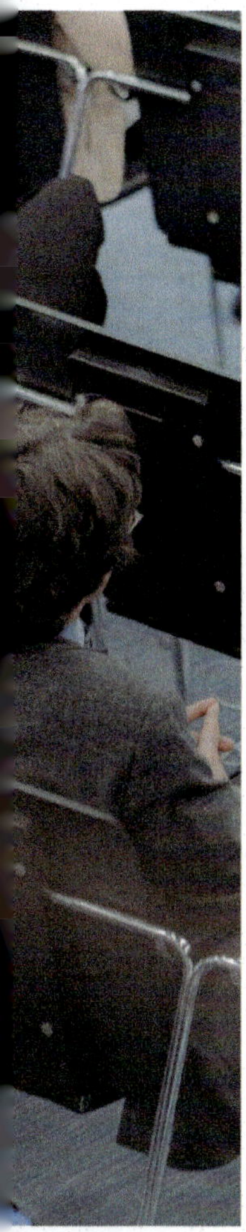

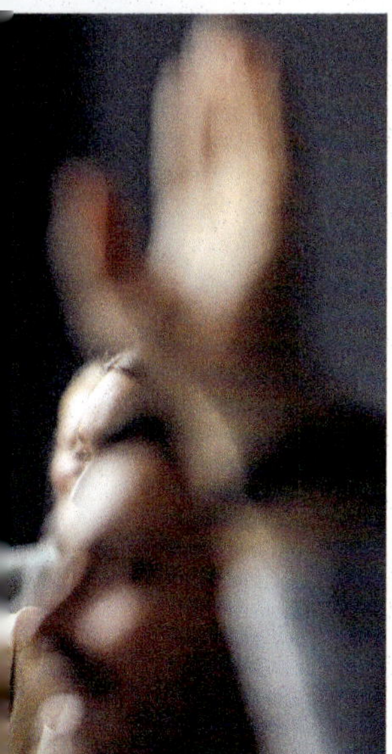

The whole picture: empowering the learner

Within our discussions we agreed that empowering the learner is the ultimate outcome of a good student experience. Rather than having students tread water through their years with us, we should be encouraging them to take ownership of their learning journey. To offer inspiration and support in equal measures, but help students find these opportunities for themselves.

Whilst we want to create a happy, shiny student experience we must not forget the role of challenge and difficulty in personal growth. The global pandemic brought this even more into the light. It is therefore vital that as we think more about that complete picture of how student experience fits into the wider student journey to make sure we get it right. How does a student access help if they need it? Where are the skills for dealing with adversity supported in our institutions?

The workshop provided new frameworks for thinking about these questions and also gave participants the chance to design their own interventions in the context of their institutions. We need to be able to map the student journey from setting foot in a university through to graduation, understanding the preconceptions, the challenges and the rewards they get on this journey as part of their experience. In our focused unpicking of the student experience, we found much more to examine alongside ideas and inspirations. The conversation continues!

The next edition of the workshop will in March 2024, more details can be found online, or email Virginie Heredia-Rosa at virginie.heredia-rosa@efmdglobal.org for further information.

About the Author

Dr Stephanie Lambert is Academic Mentor at London School of Economics and Political Science, UK.

Re-imagining Business School Doctoral Programmes: Enhancing Impact, Aligning with Industry, and Developing the Next Generation

Nicola Palmer, **Julie Davies** and **Clare Viney** discuss how doctoral research programmes should be more dynamic and tailored to better prepare the next generation of business school faculty members

> *Yet there is scope to better understand the potential for closer alignment between organisations and management doctoral experiences*

Cinderella and synergies

Business and management studies is the most popular university subject globally. Many business schools have been preoccupied with attracting and supporting large numbers of undergraduate students. There is a tendency, however, for doctoral school programmes to be neglected like Cinderella (as Mark Saunders noted at EFMD's 2019 doctoral programmes conference), with little attention paid to their impact. This is curious as the academic faculty pipeline and future of business and management degree education and research largely depend on the production of high-quality doctoral graduates. Clearly, business schools are major players that influence our lives through graduating workers, managers, and leaders in many different types of organisations. Yet there is scope to better understand the potential for closer alignment between organisations and management doctoral experiences, graduate outcomes, and leading-edge practices in business and management studies.

Fit for what purpose?

Our recently published book *Business and management doctorates worldwide: developing the next generation* published by Emerald is based on valuable insights from EFMD's annual doctoral programmes conferences and the *EQUAL Guidelines for Doctoral Programmes in Business and Management*. We draw on our combined experiences of leading business and management programmes and researcher development initiatives that encompass postgraduate researcher and research supervisor development and our work for and within business schools. We explore key characteristics of business and management doctorates and the implications of these for future practice and the development of the next generation of doctoral researchers. We also highlight the power dynamics involved in business school doctoral provision, supervision arrangements, and research environments. Finally, we discuss career development prospects as well as opportunities to harness potential value from alumni relationships and doctoral impact.

The dynamics of business and management doctoral programmes

Globally, business school doctoral degree portfolios encompass professional doctorates (e.g., DBA, executive PhDs), industry-based collaborations, as well as publication-based awards. This is in addition to the traditional monograph PhD. Low barriers to entry for delivery (except for the costs of hiring suitably qualified supervisors) have contributed to the proliferation of the award internationally in business schools. There are high levels of competition and substitutability between doctoral education providers in the sector. Although there is a heavy European and North American influence on business school education (linked to Western conceptualisations of 'world class education', associated training, quality assurance metrics and the influence of accreditation bodies such as EQUIS, AACSB and AMBA), growth patterns of business and management doctorates are more complicated than West to East (and North to South) diffusion. This is not least because of a reliance on international flows of students and faculty in some countries such as Australia and in business schools in particular. It is important to acknowledge that Asian institutions present

We contend that a heavy focus on the reproduction of the academy frustrates acknowledgement of where knowledge sits in knowledge economies

some of the most significant challenges to the existing 'business school global order' currently dominated by North American and European institutions such as Columbia, INSEAD, London Business School, MIT Sloan, and Stanford. In what has been called the 'Asian century' the significance of the appeal of North American research environments as places for East Asian graduate students to pursue research careers has often been overlooked. It has been estimated that almost 90% of business school faculty in South Korea hold US social science PhDs. Academics who return from studying in countries with established reputations for delivering high quality doctoral education such as the USA often, by default, gain prestige.

This landscape contributes to perpetuating an elite, research-intensive model of doctoral education with conservative business school norms and values which are reproduced in the academy. There is a dichotomy between reported shortages of business school faculty and academic employment opportunities for business school doctoral graduates. Despite this, many business and management doctoral programmes are inherently infused with the idea of academic prestige. It is interesting to ask which business schools have generated a model of doctoral graduate skills and competences desired by businesses? There is scope for further exploration and sharing of practice to understand what doctoral training meets the changing expectations and needs of business school doctorate stakeholders and other key interested parties to ensure that business school doctorates are contributing to the UN's Sustainable Development Goals and networks such as Responsible Research for Business and Management.

A need to globalise education and research programmes to be competitive is founded on commonly shared expectations that a small number of leading universities will dominate global higher education. The potential to achieve foreign policy goals (not least in terms of country image) is recognised through what Crowley-Vigneau *et al.* (2022:12) call "embracing the international norm on world-class universities," and international expansion of business schools is associated with attempts to compete for influence across global markets and exploit the soft power benefits of internationalised higher education systems. Indeed, we are witnessing the adoption of Western models of doctoral management in non-Western contexts and the influence of elite Anglophone business schools is especially notable. We contend that a heavy focus on the reproduction of the academy frustrates acknowledgement of where knowledge sits in knowledge economies. It fails to exploit the potential role of the doctorate within management education portfolios to offer a wider impact on society for economic development and innovation in a volatile, uncertain, complex and ambiguous (VUCA) world as we grapple with the United Nations' Sustainable Development Goals and note the January 2023 AACSB White Paper guidance.

Indeterminate routes?

New routes to doctorates have, in some institutions, generated tensions and pitting of the (historically accepted monograph) PhD against the DBA, executive PhD and publication-based PhD. Not all business schools offer a DBA or practice-focused doctorate for example despite a continued focus on the MBA as a prestigious and legitimised award. There are differences in perceived status between types of doctorate, and the business and management (monograph) PhD has its legacy as the 'prized cow' or pedigree. This is despite the DBA pre-dating the PhD at Harvard University when in 1953 Harvard Business School was not authorised to award a PhD (Bogle, 2019).

There is scope to extend exploration of practice-based and work-based learning approaches beyond business and management PhD and DBA scholarship in academic outputs. This is important to demonstrate impact in organisations and society more widely. It also matters to enhance the legitimacy of business schools and business school doctorates in multiple domains including policy, public organisations, private firms, entrepreneurship and different types of organisations and sectors beyond academia, and depends on the 'openness' of business schools and business.

A focus on executive education reflects a trend towards business school redefinitions of organisational identity in an entrepreneurial sense and may be seen as part of repositioning the business school to meet industry needs more explicitly, to become closer to economic practice, and to leverage corporate investment, knowledge, and innovation. For prospective candidates, in 2018 Columbia Southern University outlined four benefits of DBA study: 'bolstered credibility'; 'expanded career opportunities'; 'greater opportunities for promotion'; and 'better potential for higher salaries'. Similarly, outside the USA, the value of the doctorate to candidates who already enjoy executive employment is often promoted in terms of career advancement. However, little is known about the impact of DBA completion on management practice. Well-established and experienced end of career individuals may embark on a DBA to exit a full-time career path and to follow a portfolio career path (including consultancy, advisory, voluntary work), to step off a career treadmill rather than rise within the ranks. There is however, scope for more systematic data collection on attrition rates given that domestic and overseas DBA attrition rates per year in Australia have been estimated at 17% and 13% (Kortt *et al.*, 2016) and comparator data over time and between countries is lacking.

The price of knowledge

The positioning of some business and management doctoral awards such as the DBA as 'executive education' for 'senior level' managers may result in premium pricing. At Cambridge Judge Business School, the 2021 entry fee for the Business Doctorate (BusD) was £80,000 for the first year and £50,000 p.a. for the following three years , i.e. £230,000 (€268,548) in total. Curiously, in 2021 the Cambridge University website listed only three current doctoral researchers on the BusD – three male candidates supervised by three male professors. Clearly, this niche is highly exclusive where there is a strong brand! Nevertheless, within the doctorate as a business school 'Cinderella' scenario, heads of universities may be aware of premium-priced DBAs as a ready source of income.

High fee levels can place pressure on programme managers of business school doctorates and particularly raise questions about the offer and its value and how completions can be achieved when candidates may be time-strapped executives being supervised by someone who may be perceived as less qualified and experienced.

Fee levels inevitably restrict talent pool access. Who can afford a £230,000 DBA or the £20,000 a year PhD fees for international students charged by some Australian, USA and Asian business schools? What does this signal for the achievement of diversity, equity, inclusion and belonging, in line with accreditation body criteria such as AACSB? There is much to reflect on in terms of business school doctoral recruitment and selection processes representing the picking of winners or backing of favourites. Postgraduate research student recruitment in business schools is often seen as an academic capacity-building activity which risks reproducing inequalities in the academy and society more broadly.

Although business schools may be well positioned to enable changes to address gender and racial discrimination in corporations, boasts about international diversity should not be used as a 'proxy for racial diversity' (Ethier, 2022). The importance of mentoring students

from diverse backgrounds before they apply for doctoral programmes has been highlighted as an option to improve transparency and overcome homophily in graduate admissions, especially for candidates who might not have considered doctoral study as an option. There is scope for business schools to collaborate to create new talent pools and research networks. Clearly, there are also issues about race and the ethnic composition of faculty members and how faculty search and appointment committees make hiring decisions to enhance diversity.

We cannot overlook exogenous forces which influence who applies to which programmes and why. Who benefits from the privilege of employer funding or government sponsorship? Who has access to the cultural capital associated with navigating a competitive academic applications process? Who benefits from opportunities to apply for fully funded scholarships (without having to pay for home to international fee differentials)? Despite an appetite for internationalising business school doctorate programmes and an opportunity to celebrate 'brain gain', fees and funding structures do not always support the mobility of self-funded international candidates in particular with generous scholarships and hardship funds.

> *High fee levels can place pressure on programme managers of business school doctorates*

Integration and identity in business school doctoral communities

Integration into doctoral communities is variable. Preparedness for entry to doctoral studies is often overlooked and under-appreciated in expectations relating to time taken to complete. Repeated calls for critical and reflexive institutional transformation of business and management schools have been made. The influence of entrenched white, masculine, and heteronormative values of business schools appear to contribute, at least partially, to a wider prevalent academic culture where gender issues are perceived as individualised rather than structural. This can present contrasting environments for industry-based DBA or PhD candidates, in particular, and impacts not only on academic socialisation but deeper-seated doctoral candidate identity. Perceptions of being part of a doctoral community and progressing through the same doctoral lifecycle can easily differ between doctoral candidates based in a business school context. Faculty enrolled on doctorates, particularly when they have been required to study for a part-time PhD or DBA as part of upskilling measures to meet accreditation targets may readily understand business school research environments but not identify with programme peers. This can frustrate the community-building aspirations of many doctoral programme leaders in business schools.

Providing opportunities for business school doctoral candidates to engage in discipline-level networks through research workshops and conferences, special interest groups (SIGs), and become independent learners in a particular field often falls on doctoral supervisors as potential role models and mentors influencing the professional researcher identity formation of their candidates. For under-represented groups, a lack of appreciation and understanding of struggles faced may leave candidates unable to "enact identities that are valued by their mentors" (Hall and Burns, 2009:49) which results in marginalisation. This can be seen to be problematic in business schools where a lack of diversity of faculty and/or heteronormative, gendered, and racialised research environments often dominate.

The 'way things are done' is susceptible to the bounded discretion of supervisors and examiners and the accommodation of new approaches, creativity and innovative methods. We cannot overlook the existence of conservative culture in business schools and resistance to progressive agendas that are viewed as "antithetical to free-market enterprise" (Jordan Peterson cited in Rhodes, 2022:1). Furthermore, there remains significant scope to mitigate gender inequalities in business education and to involve more women in business schools in research with impact. This also applies at doctoral level study in business schools.

Career pathways of business school doctoral candidates

More understanding of professional candidates in business schools is needed in terms of graduate outcomes. A candidate who takes two or three years off from working in financial services in the City of London to complete a PhD in finance and then returns to a highly paid job in the City would clearly be in a very different situation from a self-funded young candidate from a developing country who is relying on financial support from multiple family members and working several jobs. Moreover, financial prospects post-graduation might also affect morale. We are also aware that doctoral supervisors from whom candidates might solicit career advice do not tend to be business school faculty members with the greatest levels of non-academic employment experience.

There are some candidates who are completing the DBA to enhance their status, as a hobby, or to give them and their family some time to gain a visa to live and study abroad. These candidates may have limited, if any, expectations about the business school facilitating a career move for them in the same way that a full-time PhD student who wishes to be a full-time academic might expect their supervisor to help them gain their first academic job. For instance, government funded civil servants on DBAs may feel that internal promotion will be guaranteed when they complete their DBA. Long-serving CEOs pre-retirement who feel stale in the saddle may see the DBA as a sabbatical. The DBA may enable them to wind down before leaving their organisations or handing over a family firm to a successor without the expectation of career advancement.

In contrast, it might be assumed that others with aspirations for promotion are able to figure out their own next steps with the help of an executive search firm consultant or private coach. Why include careers advice at all then in a business school for DBA candidates, especially if they continue to work?

We suggest this approach ignores the considerable talent amongst DBA candidates in an age of lifelong learning and the increasing scholarly research impact agenda. Rather than letting their DBA graduates fend for

themselves, we argue that careers services should be available to counsel DBA candidates throughout and beyond their studies, if not prior to programme application. Additionally, lack of support for DBA candidates can result in many lost in the system who never graduate.

PhD candidate in-programme exposure to business school faculty members with experience of practice may be limited by doctoral award policies and regulations. This can impact on career role-modelling. Yet, some business and management PhD graduates do seek to work in industry (across a variety of sectors). It is surprising that there is a lack of systematic data to track business school PhD graduate destinations outside academia. This would provide potential quick wins in securing business school and university-wide benefits linked to this highly-qualified alumni group in industry.

we have emphasised the importance of facilitating integration, identity formation and impact with meaningful careers

Next generation business school faculty and beyond

In re-imagining more dynamic and fit-for-purpose business and management doctoral programmes, we emphasise the importance of facilitating integration, identity formation and impact with meaningful careers. In seeking to nurture doctoral researchers for the next generation of business school faculty members, we call for more innovative and inclusive approaches to recognise the successes of business school doctorates worldwide and absorptive capacity for doctoral graduates in business, academia and beyond. We look forward to discussing this further with the EFMD doctoral community.

gf

About the Authors

Dr Nicola Palmer is Head of Doctoral Training at Sheffield Hallam University and Co-lead of the Centre for Advanced Scholarship in Management Education at the University of York.

Professor Julie Davies is Director of the MBA Health programme at University College London.

Clare Viney is Chief Executive Officer at CRAC/Vitae, Cambridge, UK.

References:

Bogle, D. (2019). Personal communication with Julie Davies, July 15, 2019.

Crowley-Vigneau, A., A.A. Baykovand, E. Kalyuzhnova (2022) "That'll teach them": Investigating the soft power conversion model through the case of Russian higher education. Vysshee obrazovanie v Rossii [Higher Education in Russia], 31*(1) pp.120-140*

Ethier, M. (2022). B-schools: Leading or struggling on gender & race diversity? Poets & Quants, March 22

Hall, L. and L. Burns (2009) Identity development and mentoring in doctoral education. Harvard Educational Review, 79*(1) pp.49-70*

Kortt, M. A., S.J. Pervan and O. Hogan (2016) The rise and fall of the Australian DBA. Education+Training, 58*(4) pp.390-408*

Rhodes, C. (2022) 'Woke' business schools? The reality is quite the opposite. Times Higher Education, February 3, 2022. Retrieved March 25, 2023 from https://www.timeshighereducation.com/blog/woke-business-schools-reality-quite-opposite/

Further information:

A copy of our book is available here: https://books.emeraldinsight.com/page/detail/business-and-management-doctorates-world-wide/?k=9781789735000

A podcast with the authors recorded by Nova School of Business & Economics is available here: https://www.youtube.com/watch?v=unVVzw6dYj8

Get in the loop – create the future of business education

Andrew Crisp discusses the way forward for business education and how the future could look

Playing at the High School prom in the first Back to the Future movie, Marty McFly, the main character, launches into a rendition of Johnny B. Goode, but ends up with a guitar solo the likes of which had not been seen in the 1950s. Recovering his poise, Marty goes to the microphone and says, "I guess you guys aren't ready for that yet. But your kids are gonna love it."

Predicting the future is a tricky business, but it's almost certain that tomorrow's business students will want something different from what has been delivered in the past twenty years. So, what does the future hold for business education? It's about more than adjustments made in the wake of Covid. Although the pandemic may have transformed attitudes to online learning, change in business education was already in the system, driven by a host of different factors.

The good news is that "The future of business schools is bright, but only if they are willing to adapt and change," at least that's the view of Bard, the Google AI tool. It almost feels as though Bard has a sense of humour – with AI having the potential to transform so much of our lives, including learning, it can still offer reassurance to business schools that they have a future.

There are many reasons to think that Bard is on to something. UNESCO has forecast that the number of tertiary students worldwide is estimated to grow from 214.1 million in 2015 to 594.1 million by 2040.

However, this masks the challenges that business education is facing. Not all those new tertiary students will be traditional young degree takers. Not all will want to study the subjects that have been successfully taught for the past 20 years. Not all will want to study full-time on campus. Not all will want to study with a traditional academic institution.

You don't have to go too far back to see the future. In 2017, the McKinsey Global Institute commented that "Workers of the future will spend more time on activities that machines are less capable of, such as managing people, applying expertise, and communicating with others. The skills and capabilities required will also shift, requiring more social and emotional skills and more advanced cognitive capabilities, such as logical reasoning and creativity."

Add in the fact that people are living longer and continuing to worker later into their lives, and the need to reskill or upskill becomes clear if people are to remain in employment. For business schools, flexibility will be the key to embracing this audience, providing mid-career professionals with non-degree options that fit around their work and family commitments. A full-time degree won't be an option in most cases nor for most will it offer the return needed to justify the investment required.

For employers, there will also be a drive towards just-in-time learning. Interviewed three years ago for the CarringtonCrisp/LinkedIn report 'The future of lifelong and executive education', Thami Ghorfi, dean at ESCA Business School in Morocco said "Corporate needs are evolving very quickly in turbulence, needs are not clear yet, but just like a tango, they are moving forward."

At times it's difficult for employers to know what they need – blockchain, metaverse, AI or perhaps a potential new technology just around the corner. Employer needs are changing suddenly just as the tango changes direction, perhaps more than anything else they will seek flexibility from learning providers.

Employers will seek to work with business schools who can react quickly to meet their needs, providing customised solutions rather than off-the-shelf products and delivery that doesn't involve staff being away from their place of work for lengthy periods. It's not that campuses are going to be empty, but turnover of learners is likely to be quicker with on campus study interspersed with online learning.

Even for traditional younger degree takers, flexibility will be essential. The next generation of young learners have grown up with digital – none of LinkedIn, Facebook, Twitter (now X) nor Weibo is more than 20 years old. Tomorrow's learners may not want to study fully online, but will expect digital learning to be part of their university experience even when they study full-time on campus.

Those same learners will also want to study different things. In the latest Tomorrow's Masters report, accountancy is only considered the 20th most popular subject, with many learners, rightly or wrongly, perceiving that accountancy jobs may be among those swallowed up by technology.

Not surprisingly, the same future learners are keen to study technology-related subjects with everything from AI to Digital Transformation and Data Analytics to Digital Marketing frequently found in the top ten of most attractive subjects. However, it's not just technology that is increasingly popular.

Last year's Tomorrow's MBA found Climate Change as the eighth most valued topic in an MBA. Alongside interest in sustainability issues, there is an expectation from around seven in ten prospective MBAs that ethical leadership, responsible management and diversity, equality and inclusion would all feature in their studies.

The journal '*Organization*' recently published an article titled '*The good business-school*' with the authors suggesting that "The good business school, as we conceive of it, is one that is both public and democratic in its purpose, and that serves society by educating citizens and creating knowledge that leads to shared prosperity, social equality and human flourishing."[1]

In their 2019 report, Principles for Purposeful Businesses, the British Academy, commented "We concluded that the purpose of business is to solve the problems of people and planet profitably."[2] Whether it is the next generation of students, academics or those thinking about the future of business, a new agenda is emerging for business education.

At the Chartered ABS Annual Conference in November 2023, delegates in one session debated how to change the perception of business schools. For some there was a sense that schools have become isolated, stuck in silos without connections to faculty across their universities let alone the outside world.

There is a risk for business schools that the demands of their parent universities for income to support wider university missions means they become conservative in their outlook. Instead of looking to the future, business schools continue to focus on the past and what has worked before, just when they need to become risk-takers.

20 years

The next generation of young learners have grown up with digital – none of LinkedIn, Facebook, Twitter (now X) nor Weibo is more than 20 years old

About a decade ago, Stanford University ran an exercise that could have been taken from a Back to the Future movie. Travelling into the future, they looked back to recent years and suggested it was a time of reinvention of traditional university education.

The project formulated the idea of the 'loop university', an approach that saw the ending of divides between work and learning. Some people would choose to go from school direct into the workplace returning to study when they felt they needed it in the future, others would take a more traditional route going straight to university, although not necessarily completing a degree in a linear fashion. The project also suggested the end of alumni as students would not reach a point where they stopped studying. The project concluded that "Stanford isn't a time in your life, it's a lifetime."[3]

So, what is the future of business education? Flexible, collaborative, branded, sustainable and technological. Flexible delivery will mean programmes delivered differently in different places making use of digital tools as appropriate; tomorrow's content might be created in a studio and delivered in a coffee shop.

Courses will be delivered collaboratively, bringing together schools, departments, faculties and other institutions to provide learners with context for their studies rather than content in isolation. Collaboration may extend to organisations outside higher education, helping business schools build stronger brands to compete effectively against new private entrants to the learning marketplace, and creating sustainable offers.

Sustainability and more, will become features of course content as well. The role of business across society, engaging in global challenges, will become a core element of the business school curriculum. Schools will help deliver the knowledge and skills for degree students and lifelong learners to succeed in the rapidly evolving technology-led business landscape.

The advertising agency, Saatchi & Saatchi, once commented that "If you only give people what they already want, someone else will give them what they never dreamed possible." Business schools will have to embrace imagination as they look to the future. Talking to a senior leader in a university about lifelong learning, the academic commented "As with all large organisations, we decided we wanted to treat this as though we know in advance what it's going to look like, and how it's going to work. And so we just need to set up the proper processes in place to manage it, rather than looking at it saying, 'We have no, absolutely no clue what's going to happen', so let's start running some experiments." The future is not so much about predictions, but instead it's about creating that future.

About the Author

Andrew Crisp is the co-founder of CarringtonCrisp, a consulting firm that in November 2023, celebrated 20 years of working with business schools.

Footnotes:

1 *Rhodes, C., and A. Pullen (2023) The good business school. Organization, 30(6) pp.1273-1280. https://doi.org/10.1177/13505084231189268*

2 *www.thebritishacademy.ac.uk/publications/future-of-the-corporation-principles-for-purposeful-business/*

3 *www.stanford2025.com/open-loop-university*

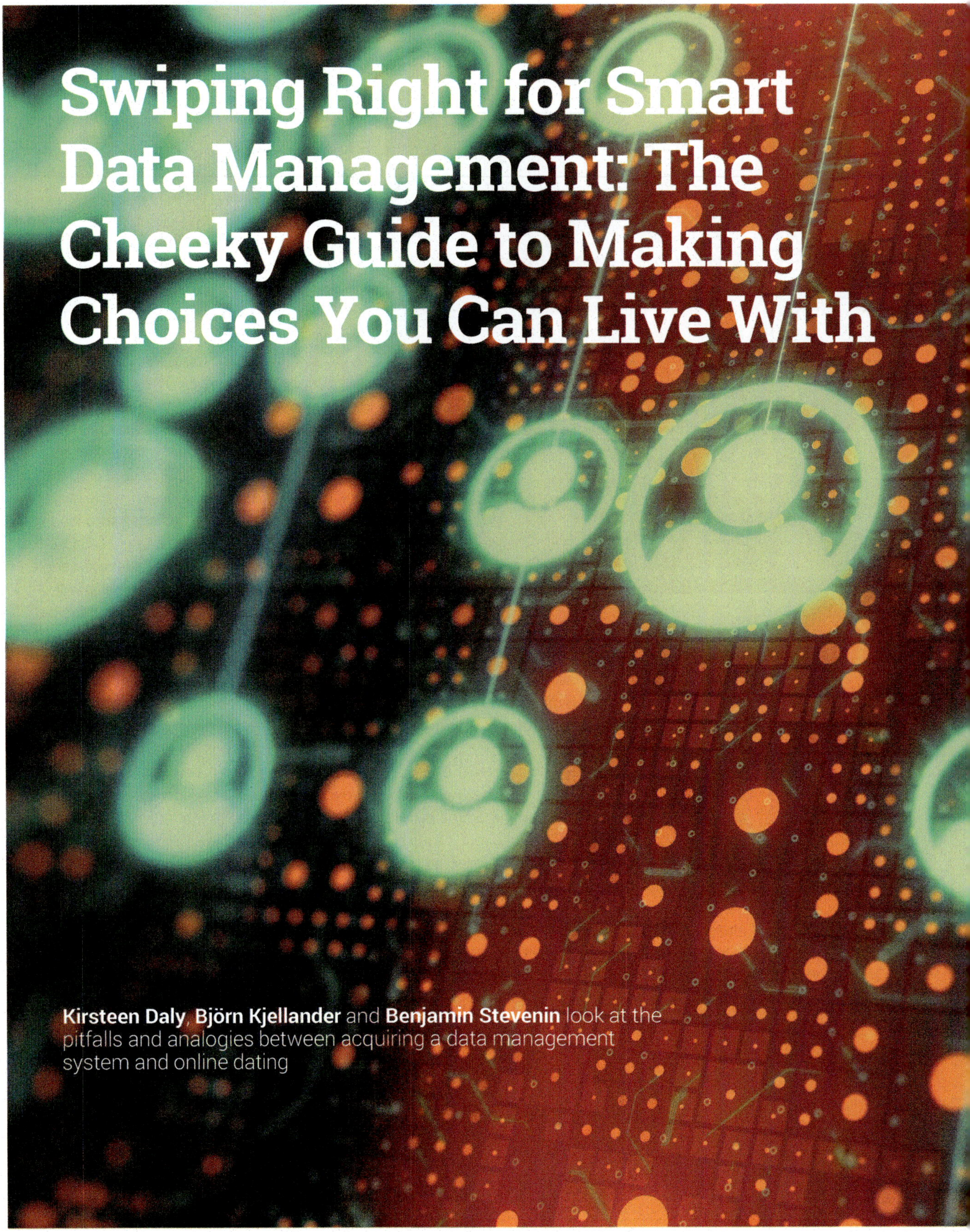

Swiping Right for Smart Data Management: The Cheeky Guide to Making Choices You Can Live With

Kirsteen Daly, **Björn Kjellander** and **Benjamin Stevenin** look at the pitfalls and analogies between acquiring a data management system and online dating

The name of the game

Many of us have been mesmerised by dazzling pictures and self-declarations on dating apps, and come to the conclusion that a certain person matches all our requirements, however on meeting face-to-face we realise the reality is often very different. Well, the same is true of presentations with tantalizing overviews, reports and tables that seem to address all our needs for managing data effectively. Whether online or offline, carefully embroidered feature presentations and elevator pitches focus on creating interest and reducing decision friction. Most of us are less than tech-savvy and have no clear vision of what is available in our institution, not to mention what could be useful to other departments. With limited experience in smart data management, we risk choosing a solution based on the persuasiveness of the presentation/presenter and the overall feel of the offer rather than making a sound, informed decision. Much like dating apps, appearances can be pivotal when deciding – but they can also be deceiving.

So, let's explore the analogy between online dating and choosing a data management system.

The day you decide to put yourself on a dating app, you have an idea in your head - finding the perfect companion. The same applies when you choose to start looking for a system you need to solve a problem, but in both cases does it always work out the way you anticipate it will?

Decision-making

At the very outset, swiping left and right in, say, Tinder and choosing a data management system both comprise an evaluation process with mostly front-end and compelling information. With little experience in features, functionalities, and suitability for your needs, your decision to swipe left or right on the offer boils down to more trust in the offeror than trust in the solution.

Second, in an ideal world, you could distil all your self-understanding, needs, and references into an informed and distinct sweeping action to the left or right. Still, the reason why we even find ourselves on the online dating scene could also be explained by our inability to understand the needs and preferences of end-users to ensure that the application or system – or relationship – meets our requirements. Swiping left or right based on your preferences for potential matches should ideally be built on your preferences for features, scalability, security, and other factors that align with your specific needs and not only on images and physical attributes. We must decide based on what is good for us and the institution.

What is the reality?

Did they use Photoshop for their picture? What is the reality of what they say on their profile? What can I trust, and should I unmatch? Decisions, decisions. The same applies when looking at systems. The sales pitch will always give you the impression of perfection, but what is the reality? You remember creating your profile and all the questions you had to answer: your favourite colour, your ideal date, your favourite food, etc. For the system, you need to understand your institution, what systems are already in place, what they do and do not do, and how you could utilise them. It is a crucial step where you should take time to have a complete vision of your institution, researching what is possible and not possible and how it can work for you in creating a smart data system.

Were you swept away?

Also, what are you looking for? Do you understand what your requirements are? Because, as in a dating app, when you get a new romance, it will affect all your other relationships with friends and family. You cannot change everything for a new fling, you may not want to change your eating habits for example, just to please your new companion, you need to find compromises in your life. A system is evolving in a complex environment with different users needing different information. You need to understand the impact of what you are implementing and how this will affect colleagues and other users. It would help if you also saw that a system will be operational in a couple of months and what will happen in the meantime. Yes, love at first sight does exist, but with a system that is installed its full potential will not be immediately apparent or available for immediate use, it will need to be adjusted for your specific needs, data will need to be added, etc.

Matchmaking/compatibility

Granted, dating apps are designed for users and purposes that differ from data management solutions. A dating app user would be looking for a potential romance, companionship/relationship, whereas the database would be designed to help business schools manage large amounts of data effectively. Don't we all secretly long for 'the perfect companion'? Does that person really exist or have we let celebrity culture and the media influence our views? The same is true for a cure-all management solution that seamlessly integrates with our existing, often conflicting, systems and helps us effortlessly produce great reports. If that isn't romance, then I don't know what is. Choosing a system is like finding a partner; once you have it and are set, you cannot change it quickly. It will be a painful and costly process, it may not be emotional, but it will affect your work balance.

A match made in heaven still has to be lived on earth

And so, it suddenly happens: you have a match, and all that swiping work has paid off. And once the honeymoon phase is over you have the reality of 'normal' life with its ups and downs. For the system, it is the same; you discover six months down the road that there is an implementation phase, then there is maintenance, and you have to feed the system with data, exactly like in your relationship when you realise after a few months that there are flaws and everything is not as perfect as you initially thought. Buying a system and its life cycle (implementation, maintenance) are very different phases. To start with, there are technical complexities: buying the solution is relatively straightforward compared to implementing a data management system, which requires a more significant level of technical expertise, knowledge, and energy. Both dating and acquiring a data management system need considerable time, money, and resources, as well as dealing with the long-term implications. In a relationship you will start spending time with your companion's circle of friends and colleagues; it will be the same with the system, you will have to spend time with colleagues from different departments and backgrounds. Who is your IT colleague, data officer, HR office, Research Officer, etc? How do they work, and what are their requirements? Welcome to the data management implementation stage regarding data storage, data mining retrieval, security, and analysis capabilities.

The fear of FOMO

Once we have fully committed to a solution, in the romantic/novel phase of the relationship, we tend to show confirmation bias (process information that confirms our choices/beliefs). But already in the implementation phase of the new relationship, we may discover that we had unrealistic expectations, even if we carefully considered the potential benefits and drawbacks in committing to this new relationship or system, the outcome does not always meet our expectations. There is always

So, get ready to swipe right on your perfect data management system and enjoy the courtship

the fear of missing out on opportunities or experiences (FOMO) by committing fully to one solution, particularly when we see others enjoying certain benefits or advantages that we do not have. When we choose, we may become aware of the opportunities we may be missing out on, leading to the perception that the grass is greener on the other side.

But we are creatures of habit and over time, FOMO may also turn into resistance to change (the friction involved to change outweighs the potential benefits). So, we hold on to our solutions, be it relationship or data management – because imagine dragging yourself back to square one again, no one wants to do that! So, hold fast and good luck for the next step in life with a system, it will be everything that you have been looking for and more but it will be hard work to make the relationship work, there is never anything perfect but there will always be a system that matches most of your requirements and you just need to define those that are really important. So, get ready to swipe right on your perfect data management system and enjoy the courtship and make sure you do due diligence for that perfect compatibility.

About the Authors

Kirsteen Daly is Accreditations, Rankings and Communication Manager at the Adam Smith Business School, University of Glasgow.

Björn Kjellander is Director of Quality and Accreditation at JIBS, Sweden.

Benjamin Stevenin is CEO of ACADEM by RimaOne.

Further information:

The next edition of the virtual workshop on Smart Data Management will take place in April 2024. More details can be found https://events.efmdglobal.org/events/2024-smart-data-management/, or email Marketa Dvorackova at marketa.dvorackova@efmdglobal.org for further information.

The Impact of Case Writing

Traditionally, publication in peer-reviewed journals has been considered the ultimate benchmark for academic achievement. Case writing often receives less recognition but can create a dynamic ripple of impact across many spheres of a business school's activity. By **Antoinette Mills**

Building links with business

In their case workshops,[1] experts Martin Kupp of ESCP Business School and Urs Mueller of SDA Bocconi School of Management say that a case should only be written when an interesting *lead* (a 'story' that you want to write about) matches with a relevant educational *need* (a learning objective that is not fully met by an existing case).

Case leads can originate from various sources, such as news stories, conversations, or research. However, once you have established that your lead matches your need, you must make a decision on whether the case can be developed through field research. While there are instances where writing exclusively from published sources is the only option, the impact derived from engaging with a featured company is far-reaching.

Throughout the case development process, the writer becomes fully immersed in the current business practices of the featured company, establishing a direct link to the 'real world', and engaging in practice-oriented research. This immersion allows for a better comprehension of the fundamental competencies and skill sets that students require both now and in the future. It can also help in assessing whether current research focuses on the most pertinent topics for businesses, and lead to new knowledge that contributes to the effective advancement of management practice. Case writing serves as a critical bridge between theoretical concepts and practical business applications and can help a school demonstrate broad stakeholder involvement in the knowledge creation and development process.

Mutual benefits

Inviting a case writer in can also have a positive impact for the featured company. This collaborative effort provides an opportunity for the company to reflect and gain fresh insights with the expert analysis and guidance of a thought leader.

Once the case is approved and ready for use, there are further benefits. For the company, it offers potential prestige and recognition by showcasing it in front of an international audience that may not yet be familiar with its operations. Key figures from the company are often invited to participate as guest speakers in class. This enriches the learning experience for students and presents an invigorating challenge for these industry experts who gain fresh perspectives and innovative ideas from engaging with the students' class discussions. Occasionally, they even discover potential new interns or employees whose contributions during class discussions have left a lasting impression.

Relationships between a featured company and the school can deepen, and if successful could lead to funding for specific research projects, research centres or academic chairs.

The additional impact generated by crafting a field-researched case is undeniably worth the time and effort invested. Therefore, if you embark on your case writing journey without prior contact with the company, consider making an effort to establish a connection. Reach out directly to a potential protagonist within the company, or even better, leverage your alumni networks to facilitate this connection.

Aligning case writing with research

Many higher education institutions employ both faculty primarily engaged in research, and others with a predominantly teaching brief. The ongoing challenge lies in how to effectively bring cutting-edge research into the classroom. While the case method has been traditionally perceived primarily on the 'teaching' side of the equation, case writing can, in fact, be one of the most powerful and dynamic ways to bridge this gap.

Faculty members face increasing pressure to align their research efforts with their teaching responsibilities and writing a case can serve as an invaluable means of disseminating research while effectively engaging with students. With the right support, researchers can leverage the flexibility of their research data to write cases and to develop their teaching expertise.

Furthermore, educators can be encouraged to use cases as a means to advance their own research agendas. When writing a case, there is often a wealth of data that can be explored in greater depth. This exploration can lead to further research opportunities and the potential for developing and publishing articles in prestigious journals.

Supporting institutional goals

Every business school should establish a clearly articulated mission that is understood and shared throughout the institution. The manner in which the school defines and fulfills this mission plays a pivotal role in its accreditation process, and case writing can be a significant contributor.

Once the mission is strategically set, it should permeate through every facet of the school's activities. Schools whose mission or strategy mention having a strong teaching focus can demonstrate how their pedagogical objectives are met by the creation of cases by their faculty for use on their programmes.

Writing cases centred around topics aligned with the mission can feed into this through both research and teaching. For example, Rotterdam School of Management has created a Sustainable Development Goals case series[2] to align with their dedication to the United Nations' 17 Sustainable Development Goals. These cases have been integrated into their curriculum to fulfil their mission to be a force for positive change in the world.

Copenhagen Business School has also developed a collection of cases[3] focusing on aspects of responsible management. This initiative is a direct result of their commitment to implementing the Principles for Responsible Management Education (PRME) throughout the whole institution.

Enhancing teaching quality

Cases should always come from a specific need: the drive to address a learning objective in the classroom. Writing your own case to meet this need can significantly enhance your impact as an educator when it comes time to teach.

Your case has been meticulously developed to align with your precise learning objectives. You have conducted comprehensive research and possess an in-depth understanding of the case's subject and intricacies. All this hard work equips you with an elevated level of confidence and fluency when discussing the case with your students, contributing to enhanced learning and teaching quality at your school.

Understandably, students hold high expectations for their business school experience. They aspire to be taught by the absolute best. When your name graces the cover of a case, it positions you as an expert in the field. Furthermore, it reflects positively on your institution, signaling that it has robust connections with the business world and is at the forefront of innovative research.

Delivering worldwide impact

After a case has undergone testing and evaluation in the author's own classroom, it can then be submitted to an external distributor, opening the potential for impact in classrooms worldwide.

As the independent home of the case method and distributor of the world's largest and most diverse collection of cases, including those from leading business schools worldwide, The Case Centre is uniquely placed to reward case teaching and writing excellence.

To help its authors evidence the impact of their case writing The Case Centre offers convenient access to sales and adoption data via its online platform. For many years, it has also celebrated excellent cases, authors and teachers through its annual bestselling and classic cases, awards and competitions, and bestselling case authors initiatives.

December 2023 saw the extension of The Case Centre's recognition portfolio with the launch of the Impact Index which provides a mechanism to recognise the global reach and impact of an organisation's case writing.

Excellence in case writing can also be highlighted by entering and winning one of the many other case writing competitions around the world, including EFMD's annual competition. A comprehensive list of competitions can be found on The Case Centre's website.[4]

Another route for extended global impact is through publication in a peer-reviewed journal. There are a range of journals that specifically publish cases including Case Focus from The Case Centre which has a focus on management and business situations in the Middle East and Africa (MEA) region, *The CASE Journal (TCJ)* from Emerald Publishing, and *The Case Research Journal (CRJ)* from the North American Case Research Association (NACRA).

Contributing to accreditation

EFMD's EQUIS accreditation defines research as "a broad spectrum of intellectual endeavour" and looks for innovation, international impact, and dissemination of relevant research throughout the school's activities - arguably all relevant to the development and use of teaching cases.

Broadly defined, peer review can be a pre-condition for cases to be recognised for accreditation. Some cases, or the research upon which they are based, are published in peer review journals which can be highlighted.

Before accepting cases for distribution, The Case Centre requires evidence that cases have been tested in the classroom and revised, as appropriate. For the purposes of accreditation, it makes sense for institutions to formalise this process as a robust internal academic and pedagogical peer review of each case before publication, with external input, where appropriate. Always providing teaching notes for cases will also help articulate learning goals for each case and how they might be measured.

Institutions need to make sure they articulate and understand their pedagogical strategy and become conscious of the strategic role the development and use of cases can play within that. On their own, cases will not deliver accreditation, but linked in, as evidence of assisting the overall strategy of the school, they can have a powerful part to play.

gf

About the Author

Antoinette Mills is Communications and IT Manager at The Case Centre.

Footnotes:

1 *www.thecasecentre.org/workshops*

2 *www.rsm.nl/positive-change/sdg-cases/*

3 *www.cbs.dk/en/cbs-agenda/areas/principles-responsible-management-education/resources/case-studies-teaching*

4 *www.thecasecentre.org/casewritingcompetitions*

Are You Impact-Ready?

How the Business School Impact System can be harnessed to assess and optimise impact, with a particular look at how the concept of impact has been deeply embedded within Sasin School of Management.
By **Francois Bonvalet** and **Vasu Srivibha**

For impact to be meaningful, it must be woven into the very fabric of a business school

Cultivating and Nurturing Impact in Business School Education

In the realm of business school education, the concept of 'impact' has taken centre stage. It represents a fundamental shift in how we evaluate the effectiveness of business schools in preparing future leaders and contributing to the advancement of society.

But what exactly is 'impact' and how can we measure and track it? How does it become an intrinsic part of a business school's identity? To what extent should it be embedded within a school's strategy? Can it be quantified with an impact score that distinguishes one institution from another?

This article delves into the values of the Business School Impact System (BSIS) to explore the essence of impact, its integration into a school's DNA, and the power of perceptions influenced by the demonstrated impact, which, when strategically harnessed, can elevate the quality profile of a business school.

Understanding Impact in Business School Education

Impact in the context of business school education goes beyond mere outputs or tangible results. In the past twenty years, schools' strategies have focused on performance (outputs), with a focus on academic performance and academic outputs (usually in the form of easily countable PRJ articles). More recently, the focus has shifted to outcomes: the consequences, or impact, of schools' outputs. This leads in turn to the concept of responsibility.

In response to a school's outline of its actions or strategies, BSIS assessors will often try to ascertain actual impact or intended impact by asking: "What for?" or "So what?" These questions encourage decision-makers to go beyond mere outputs to consider intended outcomes.

Faculty members often execute research projects with the intention of producing outstanding papers that can be published in high-quality peer-reviewed journals. This is a good strategy and will have an academic impact by helping the school become recognised as an excellent academic institution and perhaps improve its published ranking. But is this enough? Is research just for academic impact? For the metrics of citations, rankings, h-index, etc? The impact journey pushes beyond that to try to elicit the purpose of the research by asking what this research is for. The answers - or lack thereof - sometimes give the researcher pause for thought. This is the nature of considering impact.

Business schools have a transformative influence on students, business communities, and society. Real transformative influence is about making a difference, fostering responsible leaders, and driving positive change. The Business School Impact System assesses impact across multiple dimensions: *educational, intellectual, financial, business development, regional ecosystem, societal* and *image*. This multifaceted impact assessment tool can prove transformative for schools and their personnel.

Embedding Impact into a School's DNA

For impact to be meaningful, it must be woven into the very fabric of a business school. This requires a deliberate effort to incorporate it into the school's mission, vision, and strategic goals. Impact should be part of the core values that guide decision-making, curriculum development, and research priorities. By doing so, it becomes an intrinsic aspect of the school's identity, and every member of the school community – faculty, students, alumni – shares a collective responsibility for *making an impact.*

Let's consider the powerful story of the Sasin School of Management.

Sasin School of Management: Inspire. Connect. Transform.

Located in Bangkok, Thailand – the heart of Southeast Asia – Sasin School of Management integrates impact into its core strategy: impact has been internalised in operations, with measurable targets and KPIs.

Sasin's vision for impact follows its guiding focus to inspire, connect and transform for a better, smarter, sustainable world. This reflects the core intent of the institution and guides everything that happens at Sasin. Potential students' desire for impact is assessed right from their initial applications, then nurtured in Sasin's innovative Skills & Values for Mindful Leaders Module, affirmed in the Sasin Management Oath taken at graduation, and continues with an impact mindset reinforced through alumni engagement. Again and again, students and alumni are urged to take responsibility and be accountable: "If not me, who? If not now, when?"

Applying the theory of change and the impact value chain guides the school in elaborating its goals and KPIs through input, output, outcome, and impact. This systematic approach allows Sasin to manage and measure impact logically. Much of this approach has been motivated by the BSIS process and the BSIS assessors' advice.

The Elusive Impact Score

Is there an impact score that might quantify a school's performance and assess its position against others? Whilst the notion of an impact score is appealing, the multifaceted nature of impact resists easy quantification. The BSIS approach, using over 160 qualitative and quantitative criteria across seven dimensions, provides a holistic evaluation that offers a comprehensive view of a business school's impact. However, it is important to remember that the actual value of impact lies not just in the score itself but in the journey of continuous improvement, the awareness it fosters, and the various tools the school puts in place to better track and analyse its various impacts.

The Business School Impact System cautions against simplistic school comparisons. These could well lead to *'the bigger, the better'* approach. However, BSIS is not about *maximising* impact but *optimising* it within different contexts. BSIS focuses on understanding the *type* of impact each school has in its operating context and within the framing perspective of its particular local environment.

Recently established under the guidance of the BSIS director, the BSIS Steering Committee is currently exploring potential ways that impact assessment might evolve. One possibility might involve grouping schools together who pursue similar goals. For each group, impact effectiveness might be separately identified and assessed. Schools could then evaluate their impact against peers following similar strategies in a similar context. Another approach might involve benchmarking similar-sized schools in different regions rather than comparing specific institutions. This could encourage schools to position their impact themselves globally. For this reason, BSIS will collect and analyse regional data to create regional benchmarks.

Finally, BSIS is not a binary pass-or-fail process. Its value lies in cultivating and nurturing the culture of impact. This emphasises the *responsibility of the institution and all its stakeholders to ensure true impact*. BSIS helps schools optimising their impact while considering each institution's unique challenges and its internal and external stakeholders.

Influencing Perceptions through Impact

A business school's impact can significantly influence perceptions, both internally and externally. When a school systematically assesses and communicates its impact, it engages its students, faculty, alumni, and strategic partners; it attracts potential students and enhances its reputation. Demonstrating a solid commitment to making a difference resonates with stakeholders and positions the school as a socially responsible and forward-thinking institution.

The Impact Strategy: A Tool for Quality Enhancement

Once a business school has determined its impact strategy, this becomes a powerful tool to elevate its quality profile. A well-defined impact strategy is a roadmap for continuous improvement, setting clear objectives and measurable targets. The impact strategy aligns the school's resources and efforts toward a common goal of fostering responsible leaders, driving innovation, and contributing to the betterment of the world.

In conclusion, the concept of impact in business school education is not just a buzzword, it is a shift in how we perceive the role of business education in society. *Impact cannot be reduced to a single score but is a multifaceted journey of continuous improvement and responsibility*. When a business school embraces impact as part of its DNA and strategically communicates the difference it makes, it has the potential to enhance its quality profile, attract like-minded individuals, and, most importantly, contribute to a more responsible and prosperous world for the benefit of everyone.

Finally, if you would like an insight into good impact and something which will lead you to think in terms of purpose, we leave you with this question formulated by a leader in societal impact in Thailand, Mr Viravaydya: "If business schools are not able to reduce poverty in the world, who can?"

gf

About the Authors

Francois Bonvalet is Director of BSIS.

Vasu Srivibha is Chief Impact Officer at Sasin School of Management.

The Opportunities and Optimism for Graduate Management Education

Despite recent volatility and pressure, GMAC's research reveals GME candidates remain positive about the benefits it brings. By **Joy Jones**

Graduate Management Education (GME) has experienced monumental changes and mounting macro pressures in recent years. Besides the COVID-19 pandemic and its lingering effects, factors such as prolonged economic disruptions, volatile visa policies and geopolitical environments, as well as major shifts in demographics and growing educational alternatives, have all contributed to the unpredictability our GME community is facing today.

GMAC research shows that two-thirds of GME candidates remain undeterred by global economic conditions

While these macro pressures have created some instability in the industry, they also present opportunities, uniquely available to the global business school community, to emerge stronger. GMAC research shows that two-thirds of GME candidates remain undeterred by the global economic conditions and committed to the pursuit of their business education dreams. Furthermore, the number of candidates interested in pursuing international study, particularly in Western Europe and the United States, continues to grow as fear of the pandemic eases. The timing is ripe for us to lean in on the immeasurable benefits of GME in providing individuals with the adaptive skills highly-desired by current and potential future employers, the rich experiences satisfying not only their professional but also personal goals, and the meaningful connections lasting beyond the spans of their career to last a lifetime.

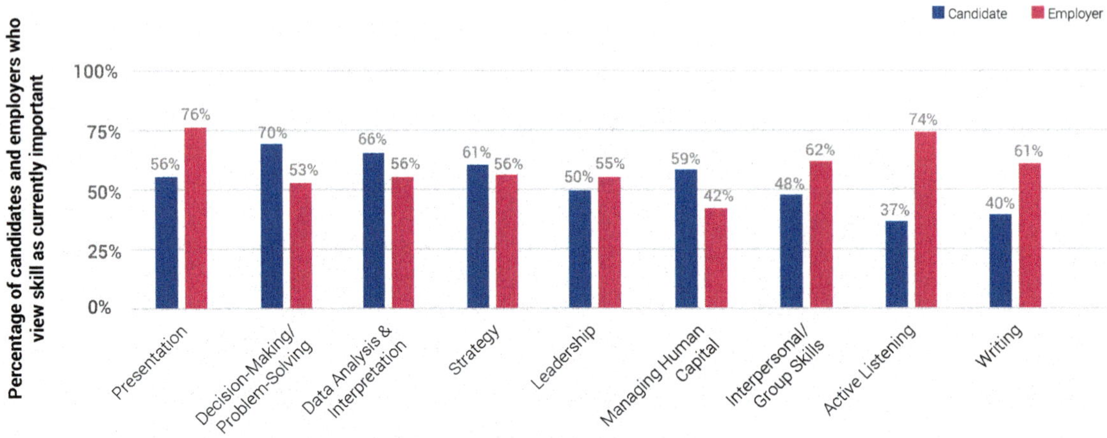

Figure 1. Candidate and Employer Skill Importance

Adaptive skills of today and tomorrow

We should look at the bigger picture of GME through a deeper dive into the demographic trends among candidates. Understanding candidates from Generation Z— born between approximately 1996 and 2012 and now the largest generation applying to business schools—is critical as graduate business programmes plan to develop deeper pipelines and continue to build more inclusive classrooms. As they emerge from the shadow of the pandemic and begin to feel hopeful about their future, we are at a timely crossroads to drive Gen Z prospective students to the path of advanced business degrees, assuring them that GME is a promising path to opportunities in the workplace that will give them the edge in a competitive labour market. Gen Z need to feel confident that the skills they will learn in business school will offer them the know-how and qualifications to achieve their personal and professional dreams.

Specifically, with the rise of new technology, hybrid offices, and multinational teamwork, prospective students and employers alike are expecting GME graduates to bring forward classic business school capabilities in new ways (see Figure 1). For example, corporate recruiters

have shared that communication, data analysis, and the ability to make strategic pivots in an uncertain world are currently among the most important skills for GME graduates – and most agree that this importance will continue to grow while being deployed in increasingly hybrid and cross-cultural contexts. At the same time, our survey of prospective students shows that seven out of ten candidates want to develop data analysis and interpretation skills, and six out of ten candidates think business analytics and data science will stand out in importance. GMAC's recent look at candidate segmentation further supports the point in that 'career advancers', the largest of the eight candidate personas identified in the pipeline, are motivated by gaining technical and adaptive skills that create more career options.

Evidently, employers and candidates are on the same page, understanding that decision-making, problem-solving, and analytical skills are essential, especially in an information-loaded world where technology is challenging authenticity. Business schools around the world are in a great position to provide the nurturing environment and deliver the much sought-after skills for prospective employees and employers alike.

Meaningful connections

Besides gaining critical skillsets, building long-lasting and meaningful connections has strengthened as a significant draw to prospective GME candidates. The pandemic has demonstrated to many of us that school and work do not have to be undertaken in person. It has made clear that technology—and evolving social norms about online and hybrid format—means studying and working can be done from anywhere when needed. This means that programme delivery requires some flexibility by leveraging digital tools to offer options for students to connect in a meaningful way no matter whether it's in person or virtually. This is especially prominent for Gen Zers since, as the first fully digital generation, technology has touched every part of their lives.

However, while the flexibility that technology brings is desirable, Gen Z has shared that they place a premium on personal interactions, learning from peers of diverse backgrounds and cultures, and applying these learnings to solve real-world problems. They believe that the classroom is a great starting point for developing the cross-cultural competence employers so eagerly seek. To win the heart of prospective students on the fence about business education, we need to double-down on promoting our unique curricular and co-curricular approach to learning, networking, and delivering immersive experiences, particularly to younger participants.

Life-enriching experiences

We know from our survey that most prospective students believe GME will help them stand out at work, but they often cite cost as a top barrier. Understanding and underscoring the return of investment for GME has always been a critical element in pipeline development and recruitment. Without a doubt, financial outcome – such as salary increase – is one key factor that many prospective GME candidates consider. 'Wealth builders', the second largest persona identified in our candidate segmentation study, are more likely to have a top priority of reaching their financial goals and earning more money compared to all other groups when considering business education.

Understanding and underscoring the return of investment for GME has always been a critical element in pipeline development and recruitment

But it's not all about the money. Looking at the multi-faceted picture of success beyond its traditional sense could be the difference in motivating individuals of different genders and generations to commit to GME. For instance, many women and millennials are 'social-impact champions', seeking financial independence but also wanting to work for 'good' employers with admirable corporate social responsibility principles. There are also those, especially among Gen Zers, who are ambitious but consider mental health, wellness, and work/life balance as crucial dimensions of their academic, career, and personal futures.

From degree programmes to new certificates, concentrations, and executive education, there are a wealth of options appealing to a wide spectrum of candidates in different stages of career and life. Gen Z, for example, while remaining interested in GME, are less committed to degree programmes than the generations before them. Microcredentials, new certificates and even self-teaching via digital resources are other venues and platforms appealing to their pursuit of advanced education. They are less aware, however, that high-quality versions of these formats may also be available through your institutions. The 'lifelong learners', who occupy 10% of the pipeline segmentation, are motivated to pursue business education for their personal growth and development. One of the biggest changes – and a golden opportunity – for our community is to adapt and develop lifelong learning systems that offer programmes and experiences that are attractive and relevant to people at every stage of their development.

GMAC and the value of GME

As a mission-driven, non-profit organisation that represents leading business schools globally, we are committed to leveraging our expertise and harnessing new insights in developing the business candidate pipeline – in partnership with schools and corporations – so that it remains clear why the value of GME stands head and shoulders above other options. GMAC is committed to all the people we serve – prospective candidates with talent and aspirations in business careers, corporate employers eager to tap into their potential and skillsets, and school professionals who are passionate about holistic admission practices to build an inclusive classroom.

We have an opportunity to bring the curricular, experiential, and cohort-based learning that we uniquely offer forward in our engagement and recruitment of prospective candidates. As I commemorate the first anniversary of my taking the reins as CEO of GMAC, an organisation just marking its 70th anniversary in 2023, I cannot help but commend my colleagues in the GME community who have quickly adapted to the growing needs of an ever-shifting global candidate landscape and business environment. As we stand hand-in-hand, ready to meet whatever challenges our industry will continue to encounter, I remain hopeful for the opportunities ahead. We at GMAC are refreshed and renewed in our dedication to helping the dreams of business school aspirants become a reality by ensuring their talents are discovered and that they find in your institutions the right business school programmes to set them firmly on a path toward long-term success.

About the Author

Joy Jones is CEO of the Graduate Management Admission Council.

Up in the Air: Insights for Developing an International Scholar Career

Miguel Córdova gives advice on maximising international opportunities

Even though you may think your course is specifically local, you could be wrong

I've gotten on and off almost 28 airplanes and visited 16 different cities in the last 60 days. Quite a record! In fact, this article was written between Leeds, Lima, Cusco, Paris, Aix-en-Provence, Belgrade, and Ljubljana. Indeed, faculty international activity becomes very intense sometimes. Even though I do not consider myself an expert in the field, I will dare to share with you some insights and debunk some of the myths about developing an international career as faculty member of a business or management programme. So, put your seats in the upright position and fasten your seatbelts while I try to immerse you in the internationalisation waters of the faculty members in a business school.

International conferences are a must

Perhaps these could be considered as meta resources that provide you strategic access to many other opportunities such as collaborative teaching initiatives, research projects or funds, co-authorships, visiting periods abroad, etc. If you were thinking that the main outcome of an international conference is the presentation of your paper, well, face the reality, global experts say it's not. Nor even the feedback you could receive (if you're lucky to get good feedback). The two main outcomes of an international conference are: (i) networking and (ii) reaching the deadline (yes, otherwise you won't be able to find time to move forward with the writing of your paper and you know it). International conferences are the cornerstone of an international scholar's career, so try to get to as many social events within the conference as you can and force yourself to meet new people there, otherwise, it's pointless to go abroad. In sum, if you are a faculty member, attend them; if you are an internationalisation officer, fund them.

International interaction is a way to attain teaching excellence

According to global experts, there is no point in developing just a local teacher career without the opportunity to compare thoughts and ideas with international peers. International interaction promotes the improvement of local sessions, allowing the incorporation of fresh and intercultural insights. Even though you may think your course is specifically local, you could be wrong - other countries have a lot to contribute in terms of new trends or global challenges, regional perspectives, and updates from international agencies. In addition, international peers could be willing to develop new teaching programmes such as COIL (Collaborative Online International Learning), being keynote speakers in your classes, or invite you to do the same for theirs. Moreover, sharing information with them would allow you to improve your course's curriculum, including updated perspectives and cross-cutting topics. International knowledge makes good teaching great teaching.

Cross-country research is always more than welcome

Working together with international peers gives you the opportunity to compare, contrast, and support your local findings with international results. Thus, business research is more comprehensively developed as well as being more attractive for journals. Comparing the same business phenomenon under different contexts would shed light on valuable results that could be extrapolated to a diversity of circumstances, enriching business research and its applicability for practitioners.

International co-authorship increases the chances of publishing

Don't get me wrong, but is it because of the multi-perspective approach that you get through it rather than any preference or bias from academic journals. As top journals have editors and reviewers from different backgrounds and nationalities, submitting a paper which already includes a cross-cultural perspective and international collaborative work, enhances the paper's possibilities of being well understood and covering all aspects of a specific organisational field. Contrary to this, if you only decide for the comfortable local team of researchers, it is very likely that you will all have the same perspective, and no innovative insights nor novel methods will emerge. The more diverse the co-authors team is, the more robust and comprehensive the paper will be. Furthermore, it will have far better acceptance in different locations around the world, being capable of connecting and empathising with a wider audience.

More scholarships and funds on sight

Think about your Department or Management School, same university, same authorities, same colleagues ... at the end means the same opportunities for all within. However, when you work together with international peers, opportunities can be multiplied. From the social networks' theory perspective, this is known as a bridge to different components inside the network to obtain external resources from them. Otherwise, information as well as the opportunities to apply this, would become redundant over time, and you and your colleagues could be competing again and again for the same piece of cheese. So, bridging foreign departments or universities would allow you to identify a variety of new competitive funds and/or new application processes.

Special projects, special appointments

Becoming an international scholar grants you access to global academic associations, international journals, international steering committees and boards of directors, these are constantly looking for new diverse members, editors and reviewers, country directors, etc. Even though accepting these international appointments would represent additional work (and this would be mostly unpaid), they would reinforce your regional/global scholarly position and provide you with valuable as well as strategic information to successfully conduct your administrative job and your scholastic activities of research and teaching.

I'm sure all this sounds very good so far, but where to start? Even though you are an internationalisation facilitator in your university or a scholar who wants to become an international one, it is important for you to recognise the huge power of an international career for faculty members. Acknowledging this is the first mandatory step to moving forward. Next, you need to find your own purpose, is it

to improve your research or teaching skills? Or perhaps both? Focusing on a target is crucial to assess the strengths that you are going to put into play and the international allies you may need. Do not underestimate the enormous advantages of face-to-face interaction. The pandemic scenario has tried to deceive us, suggesting we could replace on-site meetings with virtual ones. Some scholars do not see any difference between them, and unfortunately neither do some university authorities. Face-to-face interaction allows us to overcome the possible barrier of mistrust of others. Since more than 80% of communication is transmitted through body language there is often little opportunity to both generate and assess trust via a screen. 'In person' is to get to know people, online is for saying 'Hi' to them after you already know them. So, a combination of both would help to shape your internationalisation strategy. Once you hop on that trust barrier with your future international partners, you can then proceed to plan long-term collaborative initiatives with them. Otherwise, all the activities you may implement would have the risk of dying just after the first shot. The most valuable international initiatives are the ones that can be sustained over time, not the ones that vanish quickly. Finally, always give yourself the opportunity to meet new international colleagues. Remember that each of them has an entire universe of potentially good ideas and opportunities – as do you.

80%

More than 80% of communication is transmitted through body language

About the Author

Miguel Córdova is Associate Professor of Management at Pontificia Universidad Católica del Perú (PUCP), Internationalisation Leader of the Management School at PUCP, and Vice Chair of Resources of the Teaching & Education SIG at the Academy of International Business (AIB). He holds a PhD in Strategic Management and Sustainability.

The Impact of Business School Research

Kai Peters and **Howard Thomas** look at the growth and relevance of Impactful research - what constitutes research with impact, and how this is evaluated

There is little doubt that business schools create impact through their teaching. Many students, ourselves included, have benefitted from the cumulative knowledge base developed and taught in business schools over the past century, but it is not the goal of this short article to cover this ground.

Instead, we will be looking at a more contentious element of impact: the impact of business school research and knowledge generation. We all profess to being driven by rigour and relevance in our research. Rigour tends to be defined by appropriate methodology and through recognition by being accepted in a 'prestige' journal. Relevance is another matter altogether. Relevance to whom? To gain legitimacy from other business school academics? To the journal editors because it fits in with the themes covered in their particular journal? Or is it relevance and reach to people outside of the narrow confines of the academy?

In this paper, we will explore the debate around relevance generally, and its manifestation as impact more specifically. We will do this by reflecting on some of the articles which have appeared in Global Focus Research Volume One - Perspectives on the Impact, Mission and Purpose of the Business School and will appear in Global Focus Research Volume Two - Business School Research: Excellence, Academic Quality and Positive Impact.

Certainly, for business school academics in the UK and those countries where impact is measured, research impact is a very important metric

Importantly, we will also look at the various research evaluation approaches taken by those government research funding bodies and agencies that go beyond just using journal ratings or bibliometric data as proxies for impact and relevance. In doing so, we will invariably look at the evolution of the Research Excellence Framework (REF) in the United Kingdom, but also at some of the groundwork carried out in Australia which foreshadowed the REF. We will also look at more recent systems introduced elsewhere.

For better or worse, the systems that evaluate impact have developed specific criteria for evaluation, rather than the vaguer notions of impact which sometimes circulate in business schools and dare we say occasionally in the pages of Global Focus. Certainly, for business school academics in the UK and those countries where impact is measured, research impact is a very important metric – not just because of 'doing the right thing and making an impact with research' – which seems important to us if not to everyone, but because of the extensive amount of research funding related to impact.

Since the 2014 REF in the UK, impact has been defined as the effect on, change or benefit to the economy, society, culture, public policy or services, health, the environment or quality of life, beyond academia (REF 2021). The assessment of impact has been made through the evaluation of submitted case studies which are then assessed for 'significance and reach'.

Depending on whose analysis one prefers, the value of a (top) 4* case study continues to increase. In the 2014 REF, a 4* case study was worth about 5 times that of a 4* journal article and thus generated approximately £45,000 per annum for the duration of the period up to the following REF (Reed and Kerridge, 2017). In the 2021 REF, this had increased to a range of 5 to 12 times the value of a journal article (McKay, 2017). Looking forward to REF 2028, a top research impact case study will be worth 10 times the funding of a top 4* journal article for a smaller institution submitting up to 30 researchers to the research assessment. For larger institutions of over 120 researchers submitted, an impact case study can be worth 20 research articles (Kerridge, 2023). Thus, in a larger institution, Kerridge states that a 4* impact case study is worth up to £250,000 per annum for each of the years leading up to the subsequent REF. So, the question arises of how did we (in the UK in any case) get here?

120

For institutions of over 120 researchers submitted, an impact case study can be worth 20 research articles

Background

Government spending on higher education research and development in the UK is reported as being approximately £8 billion annually. According to the National Science Foundation in the US, 2021 spend on university research was nearly $90 billion. In Germany, the German Statistics Agency states that universities received €111 billion in 2021. While these figures are clearly measuring investment differently, one thing is certain – a lot of money gets invested in research and development at universities around the world and governments want value from their research investment portfolios.

It would not be an exaggeration to state that the traditional academic research structure based on journal ratings and bibliometrics can frustrate these funding bodies as well as individual academics to no end. The quest for rigour, legitimacy and journal prestige at the expense of a visible impact outside of academia has been increasingly criticised and has gained in prominence from university-originated bodies like the San Francisco Declaration of Research Assessment (DORA) of 2013 and the Leiden Manifesto for Research Metrics of 2015. It is also regularly criticised by government bodies and politically active think-tanks. (Dowling, 2015; O'Grady, 2023; Espinosa 2015).

Ultimately, publicly-funded research funding agencies, whether in the UK, the US, Germany or elsewhere want to be assured that money is being spent in ways that are beneficial to society in the broadest sense. Among the earliest attempts to assess research output was the 1986 Research Selectivity Exercise in the UK which asked university research units to write a short synopsis of their research and put forward their 5 best papers. This was followed by the renamed Research Assessment Exercise (RAE) which expanded the process. The RAE required research units to list significantly more publications which were then assessed by a selected group of academic 'experts' in the various fields. Geuna and Martin (2003) criticised the ever-expanding assessment framework and posited that it had cost something in the order of £100M to evaluate 50,000 individual researchers and nearly 200,000 submissions. Reacting to this type of criticism, the UK's HM Treasury suggested that one could go back to retaining bibliometric measurement indicators. Martin (2011) notes that this also caused an outcry (universities are quite good at being 'whatever it is, we're against it').

As Wróblewska (2021) notes, efforts to measure impact have been progressively observable worldwide since the early 2000s. She points at Claire Donovan's (2008) article which is self-explanatory, and is entitled *The Australian Research Quality Framework: A live experiment in capturing the social, economic, environmental and cultural returns of publicly funded research*. Donovan noted that the plans to assess research on the basis of economic, social, environmental and cultural benefits "sent mixed messages and created confusion about what impact is, and how it is best measured, to the extent that this bold live experiment did not come to fruition."

The UK, never a country to be deterred by evidence that something may not work all that well, invariably decided that it could outdo Australia, with the result being the first effort at adding an assessment of impact not as a live experiment, but as a matter of official policy and funding. The RAE was renamed as the Research Excellence Framework (REF). It has been conducted in 2007, 2014 and 2021. Each iteration has seen some alterations to the criteria used and has intensified the focus on research impact. The 2028 REF, as mentioned earlier, will have the greatest influence yet on the monetary value of the impact case studies.

Over time, the REF has become an unavoidable feature of the UK's academic life. It has gone on to inspire a number of studies of academic impact including Norway's Humeval exercise for the humanities (Research Council of Norway 2017) and later assessments of other fields. In Hong Kong, the University Grants Committee and in Poland, the Ministry of Education have also followed suit.

Results from REF 2021

The most recent REF 2021 evaluated 1,878 submissions from 157 higher education institutions across all disciplines. All told, 76,132 academics provided 185,594 research outputs and 6,781 case studies based on research conducted by the various research departments. The number of required case studies was derived from the overall size of a group's submission. More people and research outputs meant more case studies. 1,120 academics and 'research users' were divided into 34 subject-based units of assessment (UoA) to evaluate the submissions. The Business and Management Unit of Assessment was UoA 17.

All case studies from all subject areas were presented in comparable forms through strict templates of how they were to be submitted. Each had to choose the type of impact it was trying to describe, whether the impact was of a cultural, economic, societal, technological, health, legal, political or environmental nature. Each case study judged against criteria of significance and reach and the selection of case studies (as well as of the journal articles and books) were rated as either 4* (world-leading),

Over time, the REF has become an unavoidable feature of the UK's academic life

3*(internationally excellent), 2* (recognised internationally) or 1* (recognised nationally). According to the rules, 4* articles could appear in relatively unknown journals, while it was possible, if unlikely, that a 1* article may have appeared in a very prestigious journal. Similarly, a 4* case study did not have to be derived from research which appeared in a prestigious journal.

The academic game was clearly to submit as many 4* and 3* submissions as possible as they received the highest funding. Basically, 2* and 1* papers and case studies were considered failures by their submitting universities. Judging articles and case studies not only occupied the assessment panels, but was preceded by extensive internal university assessment of their own submissions. It had the additional benefit for the numerous members of previous assessment panels in creating a lucrative 'side-hustle' as external reviewers for the universities. Individual submissions, while having been graded, were not publicly 'marked'. The assessment only reported back on the proportions of an institution's submission in the 4/3/2/1* categories.

More positively, all case studies are publicly available on the REF 2014 and REF 2021 websites and are well worth perusing for any academic interested in impact – certainly for those who have similar systems already or in the works and definitely for anyone, crazy as they may be, considering a move to the UK. By cross-referencing the overall proportion of highly-rated case studies with submissions, one can note that 5 UK institutions had 75% or more 4* success in REF 2021. This includes the Universities of Exeter and Manchester who submitted a large number of faculty, as well as Middlesex, Westminster and the School of Oriental and Asian Studies (SOAS) whose submission was either smaller or a smaller proportion of their overall eligible faculty member contingent.

So, what do good case studies look like in the UK context? Here are a few examples which were highly rated in REF 2021. For context, 504 case studies were submitted to the Business and Management UoA 17 category. As mentioned, one cannot be assured that the following are 4* case studies, but they will be 4* or 3* as that is what the following institutions received for all case studies they submitted. None were 2* or 1*.

1. The Value of Marketing

Rajesh Chandy (2021) of London Business School conducted a randomised control study of just under 1000 South African small and medium enterprises. The overall group was divided into three sections. One received several hours of training per week in Finance, another in Marketing and the third, the control group, did not receive any initial training. Six and twelve months after the training, company profitability was compared. The control group had flatlined. The finance group increased sales by 41% and the marketing group by 61%. Additionally, the marketing group hired on average 57% new staff. As a result of this study, the World Bank, which had sponsored the study, directed millions of dollars to similar efforts in Nigeria and in Peru and stated that without the study, they would have thought marketing training was a waste of money for SMEs.

2. Driving an Evidence-based Approach to Diversity and Inclusion, Policy and Practice

Richard Urwin (2021) and his team at the University of Westminster Business School investigated the factors that drove an improvement in diversity and inclusion in member organisations of Chartered Institute of Personnel and Development (CIPD) and the Black Solicitor's Network (BSN) in the UK. The research, drawing on related studies that Urwin and his team had conducted concluded with two recommendations. First, an unexpected finding that unconscious bias training was a waste of money and did not improve matters at all. This led to a change in the training provided by the UK's civil service. The second was that businesses should 'publish their data, as well as their long-term, aspirational diversity targets and report against their progress annually' as 'making this information public will motivate organisations to tackle this issue with the determination and sense of urgency it deserves'.

3. Improving the Stability of the UK Financial System Through Improvements of England's Stress Testing Procedures

At Exeter University's Business School, Richard Harris (2021) and his colleagues looked at how to improve the stability of the financial system. In response to the 2007-08 financial crisis, the Bank of England (BoE) - the Central Bank and financial regulator in the UK - initiated a programme of annual 'stress testing' for the

UK's major banks in 2014, in order to better gauge the vulnerability of the UK banking system to a future crash. The key issue that emerged from the early tests was the need for the BoE to better understand the linkages between financial market volatility, market sentiment and the 'real' economy. Professor Harris' expertise in modelling financial market volatility and its relationship with the wider economy has achieved the following impacts:

- Improved the formulation and calibration of the annual stress test exercise;
- Improved macro-economic forecasting for the Monetary Policy Committee; and
- Influenced broader aspects of BoE financial stability policy-making.

Within this broader policy landscape, improved stress tests enable the BoE to refine its response to market volatility and thereby have played a critical role in safeguarding the stability of the UK financial system and the wider economy.

What Then Makes a Good Impact Case Study?

In addition to the small industry created around external evaluation of a business school's or university's submission, is a parallel industry around the mechanics and preparation of case studies. The general advice for the conceptualisation of case studies is eminently sensible and it should occupy all academics. Iglehart's (2021) 'Seven Lessons' below, summarises well:

1. Consider impact from the outset of your research
2. Recognise the difference between pathways to impact and actual impact
3. Identify potential research users early and continuously
4. Develop mutually beneficial long-term relations with research users
5. Plan tangible ways in which research can be actioned
6. Track research impact implementation
7. Gather and record impact evidence continuously

More specifically, the preparation of case studies has also spawned what we all knew would happen: a bunch of journal articles assessing the preparation and presentation of case studies. Reichard *et al.* (2020) bless us all with 'Writing impact case studies: a comparative study of high-scoring and low-scoring case studies from REF 2014' while Wróblewska (*op. cit.*) 'draws on linguistic pragmatics and Foucauldian discourse analysis' to consider research impact evaluation, noting that the creation of the impact case study evaluation process has created an emergent language hitherto unknown, which is true.

All attempts at humour to one side, Reichard *et al.'s* (2020) study is really interesting. Written by a group of seven communications faculty members, the paper draws on two studies looking at the linguistic differences between high- and low-scoring case studies. What becomes immediately clear in highly-rated case studies are that the significance of impact is described in very concrete terms: a government changed policy due to a study; the study was cited in the House of Commons or Lords; an organisation revised their HR policy due to a study. In terms of reach, examples include: that the US revised their immigration policy because of a study; that a study led to the creation of three test sites across the UK and the EU. Particularly high-scoring terms included cited in; used to; improve the; and resulting in.

Low scoring examples on the other hand were often waffle: stakeholders were involved in the work; the research was disseminated in a report; an event about the research was advertised in the newspaper – exactly the points Iglehart (*op. cit.*) warned against when differentiating between pathways to impact and actual concrete, clearly described impact.

Extending the viewpoint beyond the UK, one finds systems that differ considerably from the UK system insofar as case studies are conducted, but there is not the same lure of significant cash attached to them. In Australia, there are impact case studies listed in the Data Portal of the Australian Research Council with short synopses of the submitted studies. In Hong Kong, according to their RAE 2020 Guidelines, impact can be understood as 'the demonstrable contribution, beneficial effects, valuable changes or advantages that research qualitatively brings to the economy, society, culture, public policy or services, health, the environment or quality of life whether locally, regionally or internationally, and that are beyond academia'. The HK University Grants Commission also lists case studies on their website.

What becomes immediately clear in highly-rated case studies are that the significance of impact is described in very concrete terms

Lessons and Reactions to the Two Global Focus Annual Research Volumes

There have been two Global Focus issues devoted to research and impact published as open access volumes. The 2022 volume is entitled *Perspectives on the Impact, Mission and Purpose of the Business School*. The forthcoming 2023 volume is entitled *Business School Research: Excellence, Academic Quality and Positive Impact* (Cornuel, Thomas and Wood 2022; 2023). So, in reading through the two volumes, what do we tell ourselves about our positive impact? Well, we certainly claim to create a positive impact consistently. In the 2022 volume, mission statements about the positive role of business schools are impossible to avoid. Some are general statements about 'improving society', others are specifically related to the UN's Sustainable Development Goals (SDGs). Others still are framed in the context of the reflection promoted by the Business School Impact System (BSIS). Where there is fundamental agreement is that the teaching of students and of executive education participants imparts management knowledge to those participating and thus creates value and impact in this manner.

Where we are collectively on wobbly ground concerns the themes raised in this article. Given that we have the dual missions of teaching and conducting research, what is the impact of our research beyond the claims in our mission statements? Kalika and Cornuel (2022) tackle the question in considerable detail based on their experiences with 60 schools which have been thoroughly examined by the EFMD's Business School Impact System (BSIS). They begin by positing that definitions of research impact are ambiguous. Clarity about impact in academic circles (journal quality, citations, etc.) may be argued over, but the system is long-

Assessment is clearly no easy task, but the attempts to do so are continuously increasing

standing and constitutes the rules of the game. The other component, research impact beyond academia is more ambiguous. The authors state that "measuring the impact of management research is a complex objective for which a universal methodology has not yet been officially developed." Well, yes and no. There is not a universally accepted methodology for impact assessment, but there are certainly the methodologies used in the UK, Australia, Hong Kong and elsewhere which are 'the law' in those countries. Additionally, there is the experience gained from the 60 schools summarised in the BSIS article from Kalika and Cornuel.

About a third of the authors in Volume One are UK-based. They consistently mention the REF exercises, but narrowly focus on the publications side of the exercise, but not the impact component. Surely they would be aware of the ever-increasing amounts of funding tied to the impact component. One may like the system or dislike the system, but it is there, front and centre, and doesn't seem to be going away anytime soon.

The closest to assessing impact comes from the article by Tsui, Bitner and Netessine (2022) reviewing the progress of the Responsible Research in Business and Management (RRBM) network founded by three outstanding US-based academics. The overview of the 108 award-winning articles and 15 book awards across the categories of management, marketing and operations comes tantalisingly close to honing in on impact, but there is one common problem across many of the articles – they describe the path to impact, but not the actual impact of the article. For example, we read that folks are healthier if they make healthy food choices, but we are not privy to whether or not anyone actually has followed the advice. If so, how many? Among those, what were the benefits? Longer healthy lives? Weight loss? Was there a control group? A positive note comes from an article mentioned in Tsui *et al.* by Bone, Christensen and Williams (2014) which showed that banks had changed their loans criteria following their study on minority access to loans in the US.

Volume 2, given its specific focus on business school research makes progress in its approach to assessing research impact. There are more mentions of the impact assessment systems in place in the UK, Australia and Hong Kong with references provided to the REF in general, and the database of case studies more specifically. We would all acknowledge what Renate Meyer states (in Haley and Jack, 2023) that research impact is hard to pin down as "it unfolds in a non-linear way" and that allocating causality is a fraught endeavour. Assessment is clearly no easy task, but the attempts to do so are continuously increasing.

An interesting element of Volume 2 are the case studies of the research informed initiatives to influence two specific areas. The first is the work described by Ogbonna (2023) around creating a forum in Wales to counteract systemic racism. The author notes that the framework has been established and they are now at the implementation phase with the Welsh government. Significant progress has been made. Also worth noting are the efforts described by Barin-Cruz *et al.* (2023) of HEC Montreal describing the SEED project which is aimed at Scaling Entrepreneurship for Economic Development. If one were to classify these, one would probably suggest that they are hybrids. They are research-informed if not totally research-led, are active beyond academia, and are clearly 'doing the right thing'.

Conclusion

It has not been the goal here to recap the content of both research volumes, but simply to offer some reflections from reading through them as well as reviewing other sources and examples of impactful research. The article has also attempted to describe the nature of the more forensic impact criteria now being applied by funding bodies and government agencies and emphasise the importance of being very clear about the societal and economic value and impact of business school research. Funders have argued that no longer will broad, general descriptions of the pathways to achieve impact be sufficient for research reports submitted to either funding bodies or other stakeholder sponsors. It is now considered imperative that the specific details of implementation success should be provided as well as thorough explanations of how significant policy and other practical solutions emerged from the research findings.

In our business school experience, there have been three clear phases in the evolution and growth of impactful research over the last 15 years. First, the period 2005-2013, around the global financial crisis, in which the impact and practice arose mainly from translating business school ideas, sometimes through customised executive education programmes, in areas such as organisational development, human capital strategy and strategic change. Second, the period from 2013–2019, in which students, faculty and organisations recognised the need for establishing sound principles for responsible management education and research. In this period, strong linkages between business schools and their stakeholders led to jointly funded projects in areas such as ESG and sustainability management, and strong research collaborations and partnerships focusing on ecosystem development and issues of societal impact. The third period from 2020 to the present, following the Covid pandemic and resultant societal disruption, saw the rapid adoption of technology-enabled research tools and digital business applications. This led to even wider tri-sector and interdisciplinary collaboration addressing so-called societal grand challenges involving regional and public policy goals in areas such as inclusive growth, implementing the UN's SDGs and climate change. Thus, the future research landscape has been framed increasingly in terms of underlying principles of stakeholder value maximisation. This has generated a wide range of initiatives and evidence about the nature of significant research impact including the following:

- The production and collection, over 15 years, of a considerable number of business school impact studies from EFMD's Excellence in Practice initiative.
- Around 60 case studies of business school impact developed over the last 10 years through the EFMD's BSIS system.
- The 123 award-winning articles and books from the RRBM community since 2015.
- The case studies developed in the UK government's 2021 REF framework in which research case studies had to include an in-depth analysis of how research impact was achieved and implemented.
- The case studies of practical societal research impact provided in the upcoming second EFMD volume.

Taken in total, what the future research impact landscape clearly requires above all else is specific and clear details about how impact was achieved in each case setting. As researchers we may not like it, we may say that it impedes blue-sky research, we may think of many reasons we are 'whatever it is, we are against it' but we need to come to terms with the use of much broader criteria than bibliometric citations if we are to play the research game successfully in the future.

The third period saw the rapid adoption of technology-enabled research tools and digital business applications

gf

About the Authors

Kai Peters is Pro-Vice-Chancellor Business and Law at Coventry University Group.

Howard Thomas is Senior Advisor, EFMD Global; Distinguished Emeritus Professor of Strategic Management & Management Education, Singapore Management University (SMU). He has had Deanships / Senior Administrative positions at London Business School, AGSM, the University of Illinois at Urbana-Champaign, Warwick Business School, and Singapore Management University. He is also the recipient of several honorary degrees.

References:

Australian Research Council case studies https://dataportal.arc.gov.au/EI/Web/Impact/ImpactStudies

Barin-Cruz, L., N. Ponce Morales, K. Picone and L. Beaugrand-Champagne (2023) Empowering Vulnerable Populations Through Transformative Approaches and Research, Global Focus Annual Research Volume 2 *(Cornuel, E., H. Thomas and M Wood eds) pp.90-95.*

Bone, S., G. Christensen and J. Williams. (2014). Rejected, Shackled, and Alone: The Impact of Systemic Restricted Choice on Minority Consumers' Construction of Self. Journal of Consumer Research 41, *pp.451-474. 10.1086/676689.*

Chandy, R. (2021) REF case study https://results2021.ref.ac.uk/impact/f44e1a3a-9ea6-4ded-8671-c1314c0c504f?page=1

Cornuel, E., H. Thomas and M. Wood, eds (2022) Global Focus Annual Research Volume 1 -Perspectives on the Impact, Mission and Purpose of the Business School.

Cornuel, E., H. Thomas and M. Wood, eds (2023) Global Focus Annual Research Volume 2 -Business School Research: Excellence, Academic Quality and Positive Impact.

Donovan, C. (2008) The Australian Research Quality Framework: A live experiment in capturing the social, economic, environmental and cultural returns of publicly funded research. New Directions for Evaluation 118 *pp.47-60.*

Dowling, A. (2015) Dowling Review of Business-University Research Collaborations, London: Royal Academy of Engineering.

Espinosa, J. (2015) Universities wasting public money on 'pointless' research, says think tank 23 July 2015 Daily Telegraph.

Geuna, A. and B.R. Martin (2003) University research evaluation and funding: an international comparison. Minerva, 41, *pp.277–304.*

Haley, U.V.C. and A. Jack (2023) Measuring Societal Impact in Business and Management Studies: From Challenges to Change Sage Business White Paper London: Sage Publications.

Harris, R. et al. (2021) REF case study https://results2021.ref.ac.uk/impact/9fe66d45-d0b5-4d78-8dd9-e16bbec46ab2?page=1

Hong Kong University Grants Committee case studies https://impact.ugc.edu.hk/

Iglehart P. (2022) REF 2021: Seven Lessons learned about impact cases https://www.marjon.ac.uk/research/research-excellence/ref-seven-lessons-learned-about-impact-case-studies/

Kalika, M. and E. Cornuel (2022) Th search for meaning: BSIS nd its role in promoting business schools' societal impact Global Focus Annual Research Volume 1 *(Cornuel, E., H. Thomas and M. Wood eds) pp.20-24.*

Kerridge, S. (2023) REF 2028: Impact becomes more valuable accessed 16 October, 2023 https://www.researchprofessionalnews.com/rr-news-uk-views-of-the-uk-2023-6-ref-2028-impact-becomes-more-valuable/

Martin, B.R. (2011) The Research Excellence Framework and the 'impact agenda': are we creating a Frankenstein Monster? Research Evaluation 20(3) *pp.247-254*

McKay, S. (2017) Effects of REF 2021 decisions on impact weighting https://rpubs.com/smckay/333436

Ogbonna, E. (2023) Making Wales an Anti-racist Nation: A 'Public Value Mission" in Action, Global Focus Annual Research Volume 2 *(Cornuel, E., H. Thomas and M Wood eds) pp.78-83.*

O'Grady, C. (2023) 'Quietly revolutionary' plan would shake up the way U.K. universities are evaluated 16 Jun 2023 Science.

Reed, M. and S. Kerridge (2017) How much was an impact case study worth in the UK Research Excellence Framework? https://www.fasttrackimpact.com/post/2017/02/01/how-much-was-an-impact-case-study-worth-in-the-uk-research-excellence-framework

REF 2021 (2021) https://ref.ac.uk/guidance-on-results/guidance-on-ref-2021-results/

Reichard, B., M.S. Reed, J. Chubb, G. Hall, L. Jowett, A. Peart & A. Whittle (2020) Writing impact case studies: a comparative study of high-scoring and low-scoring case studies from REF 2014, Palgrave Communications, *6(31) pp.1-17.*

Tsui, A.S., M-J. Bitner, S. Netessine (2022) What Topics Should Business Schools Focus on? Global Focus Annual Research Volume 1 *(Cornuel, E., H. Thomas and M Wood eds) pp 25-32.*

Urwin, R. (2021) REF case study https://results2021.ref.ac.uk/impact/2cb44256-ce53-4e49-bff7-084eafa646f7?page=1

Wróblewska, M.N. (2021) Research impact evaluation and academic discourse. Humanities and Social Sciences Communications 8*(58) pp.1-12.*

Societal Impact through Sustainable Scholarship

Usha C.V. Haley, Sir Cary L.Cooper and **Andrew Jack** explain how research collaboration with diverse stakeholders increases impact

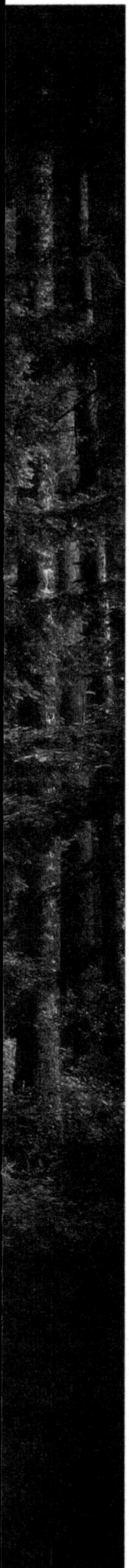

Does business and management research change government or corporate policy, or change corporate practice, or make a real difference to society at large?

Since the 1600s, philosophers have asked: If a tree falls in a forest and no one hears it, does it make a sound? Physicists Nils Bohr and Werner Heisenberg argued that it didn't: without external observation, the tree fails to exist. Like those trees, if academic research reaches few outside narrow academic forests, the scholarship may have little societal impact. Evidence indicates that business academics are, indeed, creating more trees, so to speak, and reaching fewer external forests. We suggest why this might be and indicate some efforts to advance sustainable scholarship.

Today, academics around the world understand the importance of mentioning that their research has had 'impact'. Indeed, from 2000 to 2020, mentions of the word impact in the British Academy of Management (BAM) and Academy of Management (AOM) journals ballooned by over 223% (Haley, 2022)! One can trace at least one stream contributing to this institutional importance of impact to the UK and BAM.

In the late 1980s, the UK government decided to distribute research funding to British universities on research quality. The government assessed each subject group in each university roughly every five years, and distributed funding for research on research grants, scholarly-output quality and research infrastructure in each department; each department and the university overall received a rating to award more research funding. The Research Assessment Exercise (RAE) lasted until 2001, when it became the Research Excellence Framework (REF), with roughly the same criteria until around 2006. From the beginning, expert panels of leading academics from the different subject areas (engineering, medicine, sociology, business and management, accounting, etc.) assessed all the scholarly publications in journals and books, research grants received, departmental research culture, etc. One co-author (Cary Cooper) served on the 1992 Business & Management (B&M) panel as deputy chair, and then chair in the 1996 and 2001 panel for B&M. After the 1996 and 2001 exercises, the chairs of the B&M and accounting panels decided post hoc to review the RAE processes (Bessant, Birley, Cooper, *et al.* 2003; Cooper and Otley, 1998) raising concerns about the impact of scholarly research on wider communities and society at large - rarely addressed issues. Subsequent REFs incorporated the impact of management research as assessment criteria - in 2023, impact represents 25% of the total REF score. Since then, the impact of management research is discussed openly and widely in the literature and in conferences - does business and management research change government or corporate policy, or change corporate practice, or make a real difference to society at large and/or in business? We suspect that the RAE/REF became the precursor to more intensive discussions today about the wider impact of business and management research. But, is academic research truly having societal impact (Jack, 2023)?

STEM Envy and Its Consequences

For the purposes of this article, we define 'societal impact' as effects of scholarship beyond academia, to economies, societies, cultures, public policies, health, environments or qualities of life; we view 'sustainable scholarship' as emanating from and contributing to myriad stakeholders' interests. For over a decade, EQUIS accreditation has pioneered Responsibility and Sustainability metrics as standards in business schools' approaches to management education, research, public outreach, and behaviour (EFMD, 2023). Responsibility links to sustainability through willingness to incorporate broader social and environmental considerations into decision-making and accountability to ascertain the impacts of the schools' decisions and activities on society and environments. In 2013-2014, EFMD introduced the Business School Impact Survey (BSIS), as a tool for business schools to assess and improve their value in society. In 2015, under EFMD's auspices, 24 influential business scholars in the five core subdisciplines of business (accounting, finance, management, marketing, and operations management), created the Responsible Research in Business and Management (RRBM) Network to propel a social movement to transform management research into a force for societal good (Tsui, 2023). Since then, the RRBM network has expanded exponentially in terms of members, co-signees, RRBM awards and journal special issues.

Yet gaps between research practice and research impact have continued to increase. According to the AACSB, business schools spend more than US$4 billion annually on research. From 2011-2019, as in the STEM fields, journal publications per person in the social sciences rose by 64%. However, academic research appears increasingly trivial (Haley, 2023). To paraphrase Winston Churchill, perhaps never have so many published so much with so little to say to so few. Indeed, searches for five top-tier management journals occurred predominantly only in six developed countries. In 2021, normalised data revealed that worldwide, the journals enjoyed less than a tenth of the popularity they had in 2004-2005 (Haley, 2022).

Cynicism pervades systemic measurements of societal impact. A global survey of business and management academics (covered in Haley and Jack, 2023) overwhelmingly found that most wanted their scholarship to have external value, with almost all agreeing that they wanted positive societal impact. Yet, only a third said that societal impact resulted in tenure, awards, research funding and, other resources; another third said societal impact offered no professional rewards. Unsurprisingly, most agreed that scholarship provided career advancement through invalid, instrumental measures such as highly-ranked journals with high impact factors – "the folly of rewarding A while hoping for B" (Kerr, 1975).

To paraphrase Winston Churchill, perhaps never have so many published so much with so little to say to so few

Unlike the STEM fields, the consequences of social science research have few clear-cut benefits or costs. The people and societies academics study form contingent entities, changing constantly, partly in response to academic ideas. Knowledge does not accumulate as in the STEM fields so social scientists cannot make confident generalisations across contexts. They cannot dissect subjects or reassemble them as doctors replace eroded knees. They cannot advise companies on strategies, except through *ceteris paribus* assumptions that rarely hold. Social science approximates what Anthony Giddens termed double hermeneutics, interpreting researchers studying interpreting subjects, so valid measurements must include external relations. Researchers can change the objects of research, for better or for worse, as they can change researchers.

Invalid research measures and escalating journal publications obfuscate scientific understandings. By not engaging with society, many business academics appear as Chris Argyris's single-loop learners and one-way communicators. Their research blinds them to larger social movements, while they slowly modify issues that their forests of like-minded people view as important. They rarely contribute to wider debates of which they appear largely unaware. Disconnected from public life, they become Henry Giroux's models of moral indifference

Without policy implications that others can explicitly implement, business academics cannot fully determine the value or effects of their research. They need to engage the attention of policymakers, business people, consultants, and journalists. For societal impact, their research should have wider relevance and accessibility, incorporating performative aspects from the get-go.

To start, we need better understandings of who benefits from academic research, why, how, and over what time frames

Relational Solutions for Societal Impact

We argue for relational solutions to the challenge of sustainable scholarship. Our approach contrasts with linear, rationalist models such as in the medical phrase 'bench to bedside'. We focus on interactions among researchers, policymakers, managers and policy implementers We call for mutual exchanges, rather than one-way transmissions of knowledge, and for early and ongoing collaborations. We do not assume that evidence precedes policy, but that policy environments and evidence develop in tandem, through mutual influence and for societal influence. Thereby, we argue for co-creating knowledge by drawing on diverse interests, emotions and values.

To start, we need better understandings of who benefits from academic research, why, how, and over what time frames. Haley and Jack (2023) elaborated on needed structural changes in institutions and evaluations. Here, we highlight key stakeholders' activities with which we have been involved, not as exemplars, but as incipient efforts and for full disclosure.

- **National evaluations:** As previously mentioned, no national evaluation to measure impact has had the influence of the UK's REF. The framework directly influenced several countries' national evaluations including Australia, New Zealand, and further afield in Europe. The framework also propelled the impact requirements that the AACSB, the major global accreditation body for business schools, currently espouses, thereby contributing greatly to Thomas and Wilson's (2011) third round of legitimacy for business schools
- **Professional academic associations:** Over the last two decades, the Academy of Management (AOM) has questioned the meanings and operationalisations of research impact through conferences and journal articles. Simultaneously, the AOM's board of governors (BOG) created the Practice Theme Committee (PTC), (co-chaired by a co-author) almost two decades ago, as one of the four strategic pillars of the Academy. The PTC, dissolved in 2019, aimed to define, to shape, and to advance AOM members' impact through their research, and to ensure better accounting of impact beyond simple metrics (e.g., citation counts and impact factors). The PTC also sponsored a comprehensive survey and report on scholarly impact for the first, and to date, the only measure of societal impact by a major academic association (Haley 2022)

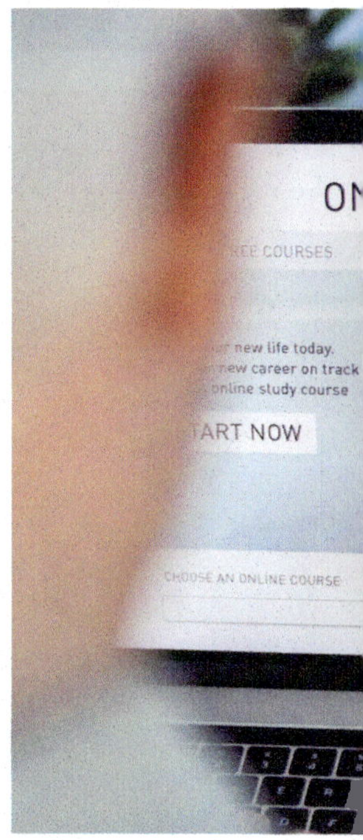

US$10bn

The arguably premier US funding agency for basic research, the National Science Foundation (NSF), provides about US$10 billion annually to fund research

- **The media:** The Financial Times (FT) is overhauling its influential MBA and journal rankings, with fresh emphases on external impact, social mobility, student diversity and sustainability: https://www.ft.com/mba-method. The rankings track broader academic outputs and outcomes that have rigour, relevance and resonance for practitioners (Jack, 2022); the FT Responsible Business Education Awards reward impactful research such as Imperial College Business School and Ecole Polytechnique (Paris) working with the World Bank to support small, Tanzanian farmers for crop insurance
- **Practitioners:** The World Trade Council of Wichita, (WTCouncil) an independent 501(c)3 US organisation that one co-author chairs, hosts monthly town-meets-gown events, in its strategic partnership with the Center for International Business Advancement, Barton School of Business. Networking provides opportunities for students and faculty to engage with governments, corporations, non-profits, small businesses, the military, and the community to enhance teaching and scholarship. In a course the co-author teaches, graduate students engage monthly with board members, including senior practitioners from Deloitte, Textron, Spirit, Cargill, the Kansas Governor's office, EXIM Bank and the US Air Force, on cutting-edge concepts affecting diverse stakeholders. WTCouncil partners with RRBM, and the World Free Zones Organization, and has won two US Presidential Awards for Excellence in Exporting

- **Journals:** Organization Studies and Sage provide monetary compensation for their annual Student Paper Impact Award to reward Masters and Doctoral students for research with impact on societies, environments, and policies. The winning research also receives acclaim at the annual European Group for Organization Studies (EGOS) meeting with EGOS publicising the research through various venues
- **Funders:** Arguably the premier US funding agency for basic research, the National Science Foundation (NSF), provides about US$10 billion annually to fund research with 'broader impacts'. One co-author, also an NSF award holder, has served on the review panel to advance impactful social science knowledge. At a May 2023 review panel meeting, Director Rayvon Fouché, Social and Economic Sciences Division, urged reviewers to focus not just on the technical competencies of proposals, but concurrently on strong potentials for breakthrough research through broader impacts. Indeed, insufficiently developed impacts could sink otherwise technically-sound proposals
- **Publishers:** As part of its commitment to impactful research to influence and to inform policy and practice, Sage has spawned several avenues for debate, and inquiry including newsletters and video panels as well as primary research. For example, one co-author collaborated with Sage and a diverse panel of social scientists to develop the survey on scholarly impact that we covered earlier, and that Sage distributed globally. Sage also publishes and freely distributes white papers with potential to shape debates on scholarly impacts (e.g., Haley and Jack, 2023).

Call to Action

Intense pursuit of narrowly-defined research has carried societal costs including academics spending less time with students, while devaluing other stakeholders' interests and voices. This unsustainable scholarship also raises students' and taxpayers' higher-education costs. Administrative bloat to manage, monitor and measure research has increased tuition worldwide with most UK and US universities hiring more administrators than faculty. In 2014, the New England Center for Investigative Reporting found that the number of administrators grew twice as fast as the number of students and doubled relative to faculty.

We can do better. We have outlined some ways in which myriad stakeholders can contribute to research and teaching portfolios through tendrils and roots to other forests. But, as the survey we discussed reveals, rewards matter. Our call includes much more institutional credit for high-level faculty engagement with students and practitioners, and for incentives such as case writing at Harvard Business School. Through sustained collaborations with diverse stakeholders, business school administrators should ensure that being heard matters as much as publishing in prestigious academic journals, for recruitment, promotion, tenure, bonuses and other incentives. Academics sometimes cannot see their forests for the trees, but they need more than words to see and be heard for societal impact and sustainable scholarship; more of the same will probably lead to neither.

Academics sometimes cannot see their forests for the trees, but need more than words to see and to be heard for societal impact and sustainable scholarship

About the Authors

Usha Haley is W. Frank Barton Distinguished Chair of International Business & Kansas Faculty of Distinction, Barton School of Business, Wichita State University. ushahaley.academia.edu

Sir Cary Cooper, CBE, is the 50th Anniversary Professor of Organizational Psychology and Health, Alliance Manchester Business School, University of Manchester.

Andrew Jack is Global Education Editor, Financial Times.

References:

Bessant, J., S. Birley, C.L. Cooper, et al (2003). The state of the field in UK management research: Reflections of the RAE panel. British Journal of Management, 14*(1), pp.51-68.*

Cooper, C. L. and D. Otley (1998). The 1996 RAE for Business and Management. British Journal of Management, 9*(2), pp.73-89.*

EFMD (2023). Business School Research: Excellence, Academic Quality and Positive Impact. *EFMD Global Focus, Ch. 9: Ethics, Responsibility and Sustainability EQUIS Standards & Criteria, Global Research 2, 75-80. https://www.efmdglobal.org/wp-content/uploads/2023_EQUIS_Standards_and_Criteria.pdf*

Haley, U.C.V. (2021) Impact and the Management Researcher. *London, New York: British Academy of Management/Routledge.*

Haley, U.C.V. (2023) Triviality and the search for scholarly impact. Organization Studies, 44*(9), 1547-1550. https://doi.org/10.1177/01708406231175292*

Haley, U.C.V., C.L. Cooper, A.J. Hoffman, T.S. Pitsis and D. Greenberg (2022). In Search of Scholarly Impact. Academy of Management Learning & Education, 21*(3), pp.343-349.*

Haley, U.C.V., and A. Jack (2023). Measuring societal impact in business and management research: From challenges to change *(White Paper). London: Sage. doi: 10.4135/wp230103.*

Jack, A. (2022) Business school rankings: The Financial Times *'experience and evolutions,* Business & Society, 61*(4) pp.795–800.*

Jack, A. (2023) Management research: why are so few of its ideas taken up? Financial Times, *February 5th.*

Kerr, S. (1975). On the folly of rewarding A while hoping for B. Academy of Management Journal, 18*(4), pp.769–783.*

Thomas, H., and A.D. Wilson (2011). 'Physics envy', cognitive legitimacy or practical relevance: dilemmas in the evolution of management research in the UK. British Journal of Management, 22*(3), pp.443-456.*

Tsui, A. (2022) Celebrating small wins and calling bold actions. EFMD Global Focus, 16*(1), pp.34-43.*

Generative AI and the Roles of Business School Teachers

It's been more than a year since ChatGPT landed with a flourish in business schools everywhere. Without doubt, teachers and learners are facing new challenges brought about by this dramatic development. But, **Pär Mårtensson** and **John Mullins** ask, are ChatGPT and its generative AI brethren threats to the world of teaching and learning? Or do they offer opportunities?

With more than a year's worth of generative artificial intelligence (AI) experience under our belts, what has been its impact, we wonder? Is generative AI an existential threat to the education industry as we know it? Or does it bring an abundance of new opportunities to enhance or accelerate our students' learning? Or both? In our view, answering these questions requires examining the roles that we teachers play in our students' learning journeys.

Arguably, the essence of what we do, hence our main overall role, is to support our students' learning. After all, apart from our research, what really counts in our craft as business school professors isn't our teaching, but our students' learning. To examine our questions in more granular fashion, in this article we outline six different roles that business school teachers play. These roles provide lenses through which we can better discern whether generative AI is likely to turn out to be a blessing or a curse for business school teachers and learners.

First, we briefly outline these six roles; then we discuss them in light of the recent developments in AI. Is AI a threat or does it provide new opportunities? Finally, we highlight the need for our continuous development as teachers and where and how we might access it.

The six roles

Expert

The first and perhaps most obvious role is that of an expert. As a teacher we need to know our subject and subject matter. There needs to be a theoretical or experiential knowledge platform on which our teaching is based. In some cases, our expertise is within a narrow subject area, while in other cases our expertise may span a broader arena. Regardless of the breadth and depth of our knowledge, we teachers need to know our fields.

Facilitator

As teachers, it is not enough for us to be experts. We also need to master the classroom environment, whether it's a physical classroom or a digital Zoom or WebEx screen. Without a teacher's facilitation skills, our students' attention quickly strays. If our expertise is derived from knowing our subject matter, our 'content', one could say that facilitation is about managing the process within which the learning is taking place. By being skilled and comfortable in our role as a facilitator, we can create and maintain a learning atmosphere where learning happens.

Supervisor/Tutor/Mentor/Coach

In addition to being an expert and a skilled facilitator, we often play another role as supervisor/tutor/mentor/coach – a role with different names in different contexts. In this role we help the individual learner, or a small group of learners, to advance their thinking, their projects, or their theses. This role often plays out over an extended period of time.

Designer/Curator

Ideally, much learning takes place before and after the scheduled sessions. This means there is a need for a carefully designed learning journey. There is input not only from the teacher but from other sources, including books, articles, cases, videos, simulations, exercises, and so on. That input may come in different formats and at different points in time. Some material may be mandatory, and some may be optional. Curating the very best and most useful and relevant material is crucial.

Bridge-builder

When we as teachers know our subject matter, know how to facilitate in the classroom or to serve our students in a supervisory or mentorship role, have designed a rich and compelling learning journey, and curated the material therein, there remains another important role to take on, that of the bridge-builder. This means building bridges between our own subject area and other related areas, and between theory and practice. Our own topic should not only be an island on its own, but placed into a wider context.

Only those learners who have demonstrated proficiency of one sort or another are allowed to pass through the gate

Gatekeeper

As teachers at business schools, we often need to serve as gatekeepers. We are asked to assess the level of knowledge, skills, and capabilities acquired by learners to assign them different grades. We evaluate the fulfilment of a programme to judge whether the learners have earned certificates or degrees. Only those learners who have demonstrated proficiency of one sort or another are allowed to pass through the gate.

In summary: We add value

At the end of the day, the totality of our roles as teachers is to add value to our students' lives. To help them be employable. Competent. Curious. Inquisitive. Ethical. Good citizens, good for the world. And much more. To what extent, we ask, might the recent developments in AI augment or detract from our efforts to do so in each of our roles? We address this question in the next section.

The impact of AI role by role

AI and experts

Does the arrival of AI diminish the importance of expertise? Did the arrival of the internet diminish it? The smartphone? Wikipedia? Answers: All no. Does AI's arrival create opportunities for students to compare and contrast what AI offers up versus what an expert's insight can reveal? Indeed, it does, with clear benefits for students' critical thinking skills. As today's AI pulls from sometimes unreliable and inherently biased sources, today's business school students need to enter the workforce equipped with the critical thinking skills to identify inaccuracies and biases in the output that AI generates. As Lehigh University Vice Provost of Library & Technology Services Greg Reihman says about generative AI, "Like it or not, it's going to shape our lives. Our students are going to look to us for guidance in whether and how to use it."[1] An opportunity, for sure.

AI and facilitators

The role of the facilitator is crucially important, of course, and here new tools have been added to the teacher's toolbox during the last decade or so, from Mentimeter to polling tools, to many more, giving us a rapidly growing variety of options to use when facilitating learning in the classroom. Will AI be among them in enhancing our facilitation role in business school settings? We suspect not.

AI and supervisors/tutors/mentors/coaches

With AI tools available, one could now say that some learners have their own tutor to 'discuss' with whenever they want. A supervisor who is available 24/7 and can always offer ideas or advice. This provides, of course, opportunities for learners, but also highlights the importance of the critical thinking skills – what's the quality of the advice? As teachers in this role, we can help learners to reflect and learn from advice when using ChatGPT or similar tools. There are opportunities for further learning and some parts of the supervision process may be carried out with the help of AI tools. More opportunity here.

AI and bridge-builders

Building bridges between knowledge in one area and its applicability in another, and between theory and practice, is a key role the best teachers play. AI offers an opportunity to ask students to gather AI-generated material about one theoretical perspective, for example, and then apply it in the context of a case discussion where a manager is tasked with a crucial decision. Instead of 'lecturing' to 'teach' the theory, for example, we can ask students to let AI help them learn the theory, with classroom time then devoted to applying it to real business settings. This kind of 'active learning' is likely to not only enhance student engagement in what's going on in the classroom but also build skills in using AI effectively. Another big opportunity here.

AI and designers/curators

Perhaps another role where AI will stand out is what it offers to the curator. Students can be asked to become curators in their own right and use AI to assemble information about a particular topic. That information can then serve as input into a lively classroom discussion of the merits and drawbacks of what they uncover and how those merits and drawbacks might best be assessed. Here, too, AI offers opportunities to build critical thinking skills, as well as other skills – asking well-formulated questions, then further follow-up questions – for using ChatGPT and similar tools effectively. Big opportunity here!

AI and gatekeepers

It's in our roles as gatekeepers where AI has raised the greatest concern, and it's causing most of us to rethink how we assess student performance. Says Suzanne Edwards, an associate professor of English at Lehigh University, "If you're giving an assignment in your class that a student can turn in an AI-generated response and pass, then it's not a good assignment."[2] Perhaps one outcome of the arrival of generative AI will be less emphasis on examining and testing what students *know*, versus what they can do. Says Kirstie Papworth, Executive Director of Experiential Learning at London Business School, "Our world is going to be much more experiential now."[3] Have we all got some work to do to better carry out our gatekeepers' roles? Indeed, we have! We probably all need to review assignments that should have been reviewed a long time ago! A threat here, for sure; but opportunity, too.

In summary: Threat or opportunity?

On balance, what have we learned? While AI presents real challenges in our gatekeeper's role, elsewhere we see far more opportunity than threat. So how might we as teachers seize the opportunity at hand?

Sharpening our teaching and learning tools

Let's face facts. Whether we like it or not, generative AI is here to stay and is poised to play an ever-increasing role in how people think and act. As Lars Strannegård, President of the Stockholm School of Economics, says, "Artificial intelligence and machines will, as time goes by, gradually outperform our human cognitive abilities in many ways. But machines will never be fully human. [...] The human capacities for curiosity, moodiness, emotions, irrationality, analysis, creativity, calculation, and criticism are – when used collectively – the key to future growth."[4] It's our duty as teachers to equip our graduates to bring to their future work all their human capacities together with the resourcefulness and potential efficiency that AI will likely offer. But how?

For too long, in our view, too many teachers and too many business schools have been concerned more about the knowledge they impart to their students – the 'content' – than about those same students' capabilities for putting that knowledge into action. Given the opportunities that generative AI has now begun to offer – opportunities for students to learn to think critically about knowledge, about how it is sourced, and about what it means for the world of practice – we see an opportunity to shift the focus of our teaching from what our students 'know' to what they can 'do'.

As we've seen, the opportunity that AI brings to our work as teachers arises in different ways across our different roles, but it shares commonalities in providing opportunities to strengthen our students' critical thinking skills and connect theory with practice. Even better, these opportunities may offer business schools a path toward resolving what Jeffrey Pfeffer and Robert Sutton, in their best-selling book *The Knowing-Doing Gap*, call "the knowing-doing problem, the challenge of turning knowledge about how to enhance organizational performance into actions consistent with that knowledge."[5] Do we all have work to do, and not only in our gatekeeper's role? Of course, we do. Lest we forget, we're learners, too. But we wouldn't have it any other way.

PICTURE COURTESY OF LONDON BUSINESS SCHOOL

So how might each of us set forth on our own learning journey to make the most of what generative AI and related developments offer across our various roles, today and tomorrow? We suggest that now is the time to step beyond our own institutional boundaries and grasp the opportunity to become forward-thinking teachers who take advantage of the latest tools.

There are programmes of all kinds to help us become great teachers, with or without AI and the opportunities and threats it brings: programmes on participant-centred learning offered by business schools with vibrant case-publishing operations; programmes like the *International Teachers Programme* (*ITP*, in which both authors of this article happen to have been involved for many years) and its new, more accessible and affordable online cousin, *The Essentials of Teaching and Learning* (www.itp-essentials.com), both designed to encourage active learning and to help faculty become their best selves as teachers. In short, there are plenty of opportunities for all of us to find what is most suitable. The main thing is to do something – now!

...generative AI is here to stay and is poised to play an ever-increasing role in how people think and act

And maybe the most important thing of all is this: to keep a dialogue about teaching alive among our colleagues. That is, to discuss our experiences in our different roles as teachers. To share what we have learnt, tried, failed, and succeeded in when it comes to bringing generative AI and other new tools to our varied roles as teachers. To celebrate successes and learn from failures together. Or to borrow Amy Edmondson's words: "When we venture into new territory … failures are inevitable. [...] But we do need to learn to appreciate the value of experimenting in our lives so as to embrace the lessons from intelligent failures in novel contexts".[6] This is important – and it's not rocket-science.

In the department where one of us works (PM), we have simply started to have regular 'Teaching *fika*' (*fika* being a Swedish word for a social coffee break). There is no agenda for these meetings, no topics; simply sharing and discussing new ideas that we have come across, challenges we have faced in our varied teaching roles, and more. It does not have to be more complicated than that. The opportunities are out there. Let's grasp them!

About the Authors

Pär Mårtensson is an Associate Professor at the House of Innovation at the Stockholm School of Economics, where he is also the Head of Pedagogy and Faculty Development. He is the Chair of the International Schools of Business Management, a consortium running faculty development initiatives, including the International Teachers Programme (ITP).

John Mullins is an Associate Professor of Management Practice at London Business School. A best-selling author of four trade books, including his latest title, Break the Rules: The Six Counter-Conventional Mindsets of Entrepreneurs That Can Help Anyone Change the World. *His teaching and his research and writing are focussed on helping entrepreneurs and their businesses grow.*

Footnotes:

1 *Christina Tatu, "Harnessing Generative AI," Lehigh Alumni Bulletin, Fall 2023, p. 37.*

2 *Ibid, p. 39.*

3 *Personal conversation with one of the authors (JM).*

4 *Lars Strannegård,* Senses of Knowing: A celebration of the pursuit of knowledge, *Mondial, Stockholm, 2021, p. 233.*

5 *Jeffrey Pfeffer and Robert I. Sutton,* The Knowing-Doing Gap, *Harvard Business School Press, Boston, 2000, p. 4.*

6 *Amy Edmondson,* Right Kind of Wrong: Why learning to fail can teach us to thrive, *Cornerstone Press, London, 2023, p. 220.*